Queen B

Queen B

The Final Assault on Black Progress

William Delaney

Writers Club Press

San Jose   New York   Lincoln   Shanghai

Queen B
The Final Assault on Black Progress

Writers Club Press
an imprint of iUniverse, Inc.

For information address:
iUniverse, Inc.
5220 S. 16th St., Suite 200
Lincoln, NE 68512
www.iuniverse.com

ISBN: 0-595-21865-2

Printed in the United States of America

Foreword

Queen B. The final Assault on Black Progress

The Ex Wife

Did I lose a good wife?
Did I lose a friend?
Did I lose a lover?
To my feelings did she tend?

Did I lose a sweetheart,
who treated me so kind?
Did I lose a soul mate,
who was there to ease my mind?

Did I lose a mother,
who cared much for my child?
Did I lose a lady;
a woman with great style?

Did I lose a team mate,
who always had my back?
A strong positive image,
when strangers would attack?

Yes, I lost a female,
who would tell me she had class!
Act ugly, when in public.
and use language, oh so crass!

She only cared about herself,
her jewelry, her car.
In her house she acted,
as if she was the Czar.

She sided with our male child,
but our daughter she mistreated.
Now she feels our girl child should
respond when she is needed.

The verbiage, the disrespect,
my presence drew her ire.
In my heart where once a flame,
her actions doused the fire.

Now I seek a better life,
a change, but at what cost.
For she gave so little so,
so little have I lost!

I was looking for a "Sweetheart"! A woman that I could converse with
and share all that I have and am. A woman who loved a good debate, was
tired of useless argument, wanted a good mate, and rejected fools and
players. One who knew how and strived to be a sweetheart; was tough
when the need arose and ready to give a hundred percent as long as there
was an equal return on her investment. I rejected foul mouthed, male
bashing, gold digging, coke sniffing, pot smoking, bible toting, prophecy

pimping, high maintenance, low profile hoochies who quote the ideas of Saints, while living the ideals of reptiles. I Will not compete with God, money, men, women, or tools for the love of a woman, and I am not willing to wait until I die to experience paradise. "I will be happy, while I am alive and breathing!"

I have known classy women, but I never heard a woman with class proclaim: "I KNOW I HAVE CLASS!" If you have it, you don't have to convince anyone. If you don't, you can't convince anyone, "But Yourself"! Your car, your job, your good looks, or your clothes have nothing to do with class. Class is Presentation! Mannerisms! Attitude! Judgment! Language! Who you are, not who you wannabee! My ex had no problem exhibiting bad manners in public, or exercising God given rights to take advantage of others. She didn't mind using profanity, and drove her Cadillac to the grocery, wearing a full length fur, to make purchases with food stamps. She argues: "I know I have class"!

Some males travel through life MIS INFORMED, MIS EDUCATED, MIS GUIDED, MIS TAKEN for REAL MEN, and doing things that the rest of us are not. Stop saying what all men do and recognize the fact that you are "STUCK on STUPID" all by yourself!

"It's okay to ruin your life, but what message are you sending to the children"?

Chapter 1

Our daughter is supportive, but critical about my going to sister in-laws for answers. She says: "They have issues that they are not trying to handle, so why ask for help from people who don't understand themselves". Neither aunts, nor her cousins are likely to say good things about her, as she is unlike them and refused to participate in scams. Her mother told aunts, on her side of the family, what she wanted them to hear, but says: "A family that prays together, stays together"! Shall I find myself dodging lightning bolts as we sit in church, because she fails to acknowledge her activities on days other than Sunday?

She took sides against her own child, who will not lie, or steal, and many was the time that I saw her beaming when our daughter and I would tiff, while my stepson did no wrong! Granny sent, him, money and guess who spent it, "on herself"! He was always right, but counselors and teachers complained that his grades were not good and that he was not putting effort into his studies. In conversation, she raves about him, but her actions are different, when she doesn't get what she wants. When he turned eighteen, she sent him to live with his dad, in San Francisco, saying that she sent him away because I was not a good father. "She knew the money would stop coming"!

If our daughter had problems at school, insensitive White Officials knew that they could depend on Mom to punish, even when her daughter had done no wrong, so I made plans for her to attend a Black College. Our daughter lives with me in Baltimore, attends Morgan State University, and works in a division of my employer! Dr. Carbo, the company's EAP Psychologist, says that my daughter and I have begun healing, but we must "both" divorce ourselves, from her mother, if we want continue the healing process!

When did this massive change take place and why are we allowing "Jezebel's" to make excuses and blame their behavior on men? Women are all over the media, doing crazy things and telling us that they don't care what the rest of us think, while others are straddling the fence, or cheering for arrogant ugliness. I am neither a psychopath, nor a sociopath and feel that I am not different from most who believe in good people, truth and the laws of nature. I am spiritually healthy, physically fit, and love being me. I love my family, my friends, my past, my present and what I see as my future. I am not convinced that all women are bad and will not take liberties as some women have, saying, and telling daughters, in the presence of their sons and fathers, that all men are dogs! General disrespect of women would be an affront to my mother, aunts, grandmother, sisters and cousins, who all have their moments, but have so many admirable traits that I will forever, admire, love and respect them.

There was a time when Black Males would not disrespect their mothers and were ready to fight, if anyone said bad things about her. We learned to play the "Dozens" to desensitize ourselves against those who might talk about Mom to get us riled up. In modern times young males disrespect women in much the same way that they disrespect everyone else and use the very same profanity that "Young Mothers" use to disrespect them.

My ex , some of her sisters and friends, and many modern women, remind me of a story that I read on the INTERNET:

"One bright, beautiful, Sunday morning everyone in the tiny town of Johnstown got up early and went to the local church. Before the service started, the townspeople were sitting in their pews talking about their lives, their families, etc.

Suddenly, Satan appeared at the front of the church. Everyone started screaming and running for the front entrance, trampling one another in a frantic effort to get away from the evil incarnate.

Soon everyone is evacuated from the church except for one elderly gentleman who sat calmly in his pew, not moving, seemingly oblivious to the fact that God's ultimate enemy is in his presence.

Now this confused Satan, so he walked up to the man and said, Hey! Don't you know who I am?

The man replied, Yep, sure do. Satan asked, Aren't you afraid of me? Nope, sure ain't, said the man. Satan was a little perturbed at his response and queried: Why aren't you afraid of me? The man calmly replied, I've been married to your sister for 25 years."

If crazy women can repent and go to heaven, the biblical concepts that I was taught as a child are useless as a guide for responsible humans! I believe: "God hates a lying tongue", and "One who spreads discord is an abomination"! My ex tried to make me unacceptable, as a father, to my children, by telling ugly stories, while she wouldn't know the truth if it sat on her face. Now, her favorite words are "Hallelujah" and "Praise the lord", like many religionist who don't practice what they preach.

Why do unaware, unkind, insensitive people always attempt to be spokespersons for religion. Of the most outspoken co workers at my job, the poorest examples of employees are first to quote the bible, while no amount of conversation causes improvement in their work habits, or their relationship with other employees.

And, there is this ongoing debate about qualities, or inequalities of ethnic women as mothers and wives. I feel that "Some White Females" make great wives, but are weak as mothers and "Some Black Females" make great mothers, but poor wives! "Some White Females support mates, while failing to teach children a moral equation"! The debate over whether, or not, to spank illustrates the extent of their confusion. Dr. Spock, started the debate, but later admitted that he was wrong. The argument is that spanking causes violent behavior, but the reality is that males inflict more violence during athletics than exists in a spanking. There were fewer school shootings when we spanked our children and less general violence throughout our society. The issue is not whether we spank, but that we are failing to find ways to connect with our children, because we are out of touch with ourselves. Good parents do not rule out necessary options in the rearing of children. To quote a guest on a popular talk show: "You tell me I can't spank my Black Son, but you have no problem when a policeman puts a bullet in his head"!

I can still remember my daughter's last spanking. She was eleven, and this was to be her third spanking from me. She cried, went to her room, as I told her to, and later came back and asked me why she got a spanking. I told her all the reasons, after which she suggested: "Boy, I guess I deserved that spanking.

When my son was seven, I gave him a choice of a spanking, or going to his room and he chose the spanking. His mother negated most of what I tried to teach him by challenging me in front of him, while my daughter, as an adult tells, how she hid in closets when her mother came home from work, because her treatment was contingent on how things went at work, or mood swings. My wife taught our son to drive and drink beer, so I was wasting time teaching standards and discipline, or telling him not to drive, because he was young and irresponsible.

Dr. Spock wasn't wrong, when he said: "Spare the rod and spoil the child"! He simply expressed an idea that most did not properly include in their child rearing habits, because they are not open to learning "Complete Concepts'. Recent studies from the University of California at Berkeley imply that spanking a child, if done properly, is less harmful than permissive parenting. For some, it is more important to gain money, power and a career than to do an adequate job of guiding children, so parents often do a better job at the office than in their homes, and many are doing a poor job at work. The debate should be about standards and discipline, but many of us provide horrible examples as parents and expect children to survive our craziness. Some parents think harsh punishment is the answer, others do inane things in the presence of children and demand: "Don't do as I do, do as I say"! The silliest of all statements is "I brought you into this world and I can take you out"!

It is generally anticipated that White Males, in positions of power, get minimal punishment, so maybe time out and standing in a corners, during childhood, gave flawed, unscrupulous males opportunity to test the waters for future psychopathic behavior. It took over thirty years for a jury to convict the man who killed Medgar Evers, even as he bragged to friends and the media, and that is only one of many examples of White Male Dysfunction. Blacks have had to put up with "Deviant White Male Behavior" throughout the history of the U.S. of A., yet Whites are quick to challenge Black Parents for spanking. Now some Black Mothers are jumping on the bandwagon and challenging husbands on national television. To quote one Black Male on a nationally syndicated talk show: "I am being challenged for spanking my child, but it is also my fault when my undisciplined Black Son is Shot in the head by a "Racist White Police Officer who didn't give a damn whether my son was innocent, or guilty.

Some White Males have a history of inflicting violence on people that they considered less than themselves and this includes beatings, lynching, mutilation, drug dealing, unlawful arrest, media and political manipulation,…. Supportive spouses have been recipients of insensitive behavior and while specific activities may not have been with the consent of the wife, or mother one must ask: "What kind of women supported men who participate in such acts, or lived with men who were capable of such atrocities?

Other males have been known to dump wives upon reaching the pinnacle of success and later treat the woman who supported the rise to the top as less than human. Females who are not part of the solution are part of the problem and help men gain money, power, fame and infamy, thus allowing them to continue their errant ways. Then, there are the females who act like the crazy men when they gain power and fame.

When my wife made more money than I, she became arrogant, self righteous and complained that I was not living up to my education, or skill level! She says I am not devious enough, while she travels through life being unethical, selfish, conniving and character flawed. She overspent, filed bankruptcies and false insurance claims counteracting my every move, so I could never get started on business plans that I developed. She maintained a separate account, but used the majority of the funds in our joint account. I borrowed to pay bills that she made, but as soon as I paid one, she developed another. On one occasion she paid a month and a half on the mortgage with funds that I had put into an account with her credit union, rather than add to the funds and pay a full two months. On another occasion, my company paid me $8,000 in back pay and she spent it from our joint account in less than a month. "Sound familiar"!

Some "Black Females" talk "God" as a moral equation, but fail to assist mates in developing an economic imperative, because they don't understand that there are ways to become successful without falling prey to a money trap that is developed by those who have "Historically" raped and pillaged every society that he has come into contact with. To walk into this web of deceit is like crawling into the jaws of a giant python where one is psychology devoured and returned to the family as a bleached, crumbled, confused mass that is of no value. The body is useless once the soul has been removed, so the one real option is to join hearts and minds to develop a plan that benefits all whom you love.

Black Mothers were once considered the best in this nation and raised White and Black Youth to be loving and caring. Minister Farrakhan once said that many of our problems with diseases such as high blood pressure were caused by loving, caring, creative mothers who cooked so well that they made grass taste good! They did with what they had, spread unconditional love to all they came into contact with, and their warmth, caring and love caused many Blacks and Whites to remain friends, even during Jim crow years.

Some of today's mothers are so into money, fashion, cars and keeping up with the Jones's that they have forgotten about love, relationships, family, home and children. This lost group spreads venom among the masses and does more damage than hate groups. Their greed demands the proliferation of drugs, welfare and insurance fraud, thievery and disrespect, yet some spend their Sundays in church. Their sons enlarge the prison population, and their daughters traipse through society with the mentality of streetwalkers. Too often, their boys have little respect for women and become pimps for females who have no vision. Both groups spend their lives nurturing a system that they say they hate, while their habits allow the evils of society to fester and infect family members and community residents who might otherwise grow and prosper if things were different.

Children learn by example. While play is a means of acquiring social and motor skills, observing parents is the ultimate means of developing male/female, cause/effect, and obsessive/compulsive relationships. It is no secret that Blacks are last hired, first fired, underpaid and overworked without regard for their education, or skill level. Meanwhile, women want the benefits of "Big Bucks", but fail to understand that their economic philosophy reduces the probability of living the dream. Our children need to be guided into the future, not tossed from their homes, once the money faucet stops dripping.

Too often, Black Women say: "When a Black Man makes it big, he goes out and gets himself a White Woman"! Maybe the male that you are concentrating on has found that one woman who understands his vision. The reality is that over ninety seven percent of Black Males marry Black Females. One sign of a real problem is when U.S. Department of Commerce Statistics imply that only 32 percent of African Americans over the age of fifteen are married, while 49 percent of Caucasians, in that same bracket, are married.

My undergraduate training is in psychology and my area of reference is behavior modification and social learning theory, so I am encouraged by efforts of those who work hard to rear sensitive, thoughtful, educated off-spring. I have been taught to believe that, while heredity is important, we are the sum-total of life's experiences. There are many reasons why our youths feel hopeless and careless about the future, but the system is only part of the cause. The strong undercurrent in dysfunctional families does damage long before the system gets an opportunity to incriminate and incarcerate our babies, and acerbate our problems. The justice system punishes many who have done no wrong and have no support system, or understanding of how to fight back. Many of our men, are trapped in that system of injustice and "Yes" there are too few marriable males.

Innocent Poor, Black and Hispanic Males have fallen prey to the prison/welfare complex, while, privileged Whites have moved into the information age, and avoid incarceration, even when they are guilty. Prisons, like the distribution of food stamps, are big business, creating employment and distributing the carnage among those who have ties to owners of the big guns . The answer lies in learning how to parent and mentor our children. We must realize that parenting is not reflex, or instinct, but learned behavior"!

The San Francisco Police Department has a philosophy of not placing new officers with senior officers who are deemed as less than the very best, because management theory is that a senior officer has a decided impact on the future of recruits. Do our children deserve less consideration?

Chapter 2

My older brother and a younger sister were punished more often as children, because they did what they wanted to do. My brother will admit that he did things that he should not have done, but my sister says she felt her parents were trying to kill her. I suggested that I was there and explained why she got so many spankings. She then told me how she, later, learned that our dad felt that she looked just like our mother and wanted to make sure that she did not do some of the things that Mother did. Males and females receive the same information, but process data as if we are from different dimensions. My sister is a sweetheart and recently earned her Ph.D., while my brother is retired from the sheriff's department. Five of six of us are college educated, none have been in the prison system and two have served in the military. I blame our success on our parents, who had fewer resources, but did their best with what they had.

My ex's father worked two and three jobs to support a family of eleven children, but came home to find that there was no dinner for him, because the children and friends were first priority in his wife's world. All this after he reared his younger brothers and sisters, because his father died when he was in his teens. I always heard how tough he was as a father, but I never heard about the man that I got to know as a father in law for twenty five years. His sisters and brothers had the utmost respect for him as I did when I was a son in law. Most of his children don't have a clue as to who he is, or what he did for them.

In the sixties someone coined the phrase "Poverty Program Pimp", because many "So Called Civil Rights Activists" turned out to be opportunists who came forth to line their pockets. I am ready to take on those who pimp God's Words. I accept very little of what I hear when people talk about religion and I try to be diligent in my observations. I am a church goer, but I don't spend hours listening to religious nonsense, on television, on radio, or from those who want to convince me that they know more about god than I. As a child I was taught the commandments and I live by those rules. I don't fear God, because I believe a "Just God" knows when I am doing the right things. I trust the concept of the biblical talents and don't need a crutch to live on this planet and treat others humans with respect. It was the scriptures that taught me to beware of false prophets

It is because I am not a religionist that I can understand that people who are not Moslem, Jewish, or Catholic and other, all feel the pain and mental anguish that is put upon them by those who often categorize themselves as God's People. I choose to believe that I can be of a different faith than that which was my parent's, or which was taught to me as a child and often, tell other Blacks that we were born "Black" and more often than not, "Democrat" and "Baptist, or Methodist", so it takes no genius to fit into those categories. Life is a series of paradigms and we make choices based on our willingness to explore, or not explore the vastness of the universe. When someone makes statements such as, "If God meant for us to fly he would have given us wings" I usually suggest that they accept the fact that they are afraid of airplanes, because "God didn't give us wheels and we are driving all over the planet"!

Some time ago I had a conversation with a male and female about the relationships between men and women. The female complained that she would never give one hundred percent to any man, while the male suggested that she was sharing her man, anyway, because that's the way men are. I left the discussion feeling indignation for both participants, because neither had a clue about how to survive, a positive relationship. A few days later I had a brief conversation with the male who spouted religious nonsense about God making all the decisions about what happens in everyone's life. I suggested that he was using God as a crutch for his bad behavior to which he responded, "I need that crutch"! The God that he fears is really himself and the ugliness that he fosters. I am resentful of self centered, not too bright, males who lump other males into their den of stupidity, but I am also resentful of male bashing females who make asinine statements, while rearing young boys toward 'Never to be" manhood! Our churches are full of conniving, lying females and some are so mean spirited that the only people that can tolerated them are children who must depend on them for mental and physical sustenance.

It is the time to wake up before we destroy the wonderful gifts that have been bestowed upon us. We cannot continue to destroy all that is good, claim to be saved time and again, thinking that this "Dummy" we call "God" is going to forgive us and care for us. We all want the good life, but some of us are incapable of handling the truth, and continue to infect others, while refusing to seek guidance, or information that can help stop the bleeding.

"God Is Love, God is good, God is omnipotent, but God is not Stupid"! If you can't blame your nonsense on others around you, I guess, you feel, that God is your only other choice, but don't bet on seeing any pearly gates. Some religionist believe that only 144,000 are going to heaven, so your chances are getting slimmer, when you have to compete with those who have spent their lives living by the commandments. Your girlfriends should stop the "You Go Girl" and proclaim a hearty "Wake

Up Girl"! My ex and her sisters go to church often as does their father, but it is apparent that their reasons are very different.

At our recent family reunion I had the benefit of spending hours of conversation with my sister in law's grandmother. We discussed how friends and family always talked against her recently departed husband and his efforts to develop financial independence for the two of them. She explained how she paid cash for her new four bedroom house and that she is the only of her family and associates who is financially stable. She was not surprised when I explained the avenue to success that I tried to develop with my ex wife and how she counteracted my every move. She encouraged me to continue my efforts to the benefit of our family.

What is not generally understood is that working for someone is, often, not the road to riches, so a job may not be the answer for some minority males. There is a world of difference between the roads traveled by Black and Hispanic Males and White Males, so one must be cautious when comparing groups, and realize that we can't continue to do the same things and expect different results"! If we are to make a difference, we must travel new roads, learn new ideas and grow beyond previously perceived boundaries, because: "You cannot lead where you will not go"!.

We need to "Rethink Our Agenda's"! We can build homes and cars and towns and nations, but we must first build families and respect and support and relationships. Negative media attention is usually aimed at Black Males, while there seems to be little realization that some females are also failing to perform! Most of us cannot get to the land of "Milk and Honey" without support and sacrifice from family, friends, associates, wives and girlfriends. Trust me, those who travel alone will be alone when jeopardy approaches, so if "alone" is your way, accept it and move on, but don't blame others for unilateral miscalculations. Do not waiver, because of those who would "Rain On Your Parade"! The world has many snakes and vultures, but there are also flowers, trees, beautiful valleys and sunlit skies.

Life is about making choices and the biblical story of "The Talents" suggests that waiting for God to make those decisions for you is not going to work. Once you make a decision, take credit where credit is due and responsibility when it is the wrong choice. There are decisions that will put you in jail and decisions that may put you in a mansion and, later, put you in jail. Respect, or disrespect are based on your ideals and you can fool some people "Some of the time"!

In most economies the resources flow in one direction. "Bandits" usually control the Upper level of the socioeconomic spectrum, while "Outlaws" control the lower level. "Bandits" govern all who reside in the system, but we tend to beware of "Outlaws" who use "In your face" threats, force, knives, guns, drugs and sex and usually end up in prisons. The facilities that incarcerate "Outlaws" and control police, judges and laws are developed by "Bandits" who use power, coercion, politics, subversion, money, drugs and sex, milk and honey and are, more often than not, admired by the majority of society. Most talk God, but act like devils! Those who are without insight admire "Bandits" and have, through wannabee processing, learned to talk the talk.

"The James Lynch Theory" (a theory that taught slaves to hate and distrust other slaves and to love admire the master) and other divisive socioeconomic precepts have guided Africans through our American Journey, but I am prepared to move forward, into the next century, with a different vision. Like my siblings, I do things that are necessary to grow, prosper and believe that I am worthy. If I am thoughtful, follow Grandma's rules and do good deeds the children, including nieces, nephews, grand children,…should benefit from my existence.

I have known the best and the worst of people and try to surround myself with good folks, but the best that I have known are family, including my ex father in law. I realize that I come from good stock, and my decisions reflect that reality. The downside is that I thought all women were like the women in my family, so like the Marines: "I was looking for a few good women", who wanted a man with insight and vision! I have a job, but more than that: "I have a dream"! So, from a group, I chose one whom I will love, cherish, honor and respect. I learned, I loved and I continue to move forward.

Chapter 3

The craziness affected our children in such a way that my daughter wrote a term paper for a first year college psychology class in which she stated "I am having a tough time getting use to this new Mom, when I haven't gotten over hating the old Mom"! The only change was that she no longer had to live with her, but I was furious with myself and explained that I stayed with her mother to assure that she and her brother had two parents. My daughter's response was "I am glad that you stayed, but I have no intention of repeating that same mistake"! In conversations I found that her mother was far worse, to her, than I imagined as she explained how she hid in closets and didn't answer, at times, when her mother would call. She explained that her mother was an evil person, but that she hurt most when her mother called her a fat bitch. She told me that she finally challenged her mother, when she was 13 years of age, by grabbing her hand, and telling her that she would never be allowed to strike her again. Her mother continued the verbal abuse, but the hitting stopped. It was a family friend, Luisa and my brothers wife, also named Jacquie, who helped me to understand my daughter's pain! Both explained that Jacquie did much to destroy Nicole's self esteem and no matter how hard she tried to get approval, her mother spewed negatives at her. Both talked about how much they liked Nicole's Laugh, as does my current spouse.

I became angry at myself and took Nicole to my company's EAP Analyst. She sat through each session in tears, so I worried that I had failed as a parent. I was busy trying to assure my children had a mother and father and never stopped to notice that she was a frightened, unhappy child? I left each session feeling that I had failed myself, because the rearing of my children is the one project at which I wanted to be precise, competent and realistic. I had taken child development courses, worked with San Francisco State's Child Study Center, and even spent time at Sonoma State Hospital working with self destructive children. Then I find that I have married and fathered a child by a mean self centered, money hungry, character flawed woman.

When I first took Nicole to see Dr. Carbo, I explained that I was there to overcome the negatives of a loveless, material gathering marriage. His advise, at the end of her first session was: "Give your daughter a home"! "A big house is not necessarily home and material does not fill an empty heart". I then worked hard to create a sanctuary for Nicole and myself, hoping that she will be happy grow, thrive, prosper and understand! She spent a year and a half studying at Baltimore City Community College before transferring to Morgan State University where she is majoring in Business Management. We completed and submitted a business plan to SBA and the City of Baltimore and worked on other marketing projects. The holdup until my divorce was final, was Jacquie's mishandling of family finances, because the marital proceeds were in her control. Creditors were intent upon dumping her problems on me, while allowing her unlimited access. It was during this time that I realized that employers look at your finances for most professional level employment.

On our last visit to Dr. Carbo, Nicole talked about her concerns that I would do anything for her mother, regardless of how I was treated, so she believed that I loved a woman who only cared about herself. She felt, if this was the norm, she never wanted to get married, but went on to explain that she, now, knew that I stayed for she and Reggie. She said that she realized that it is not her responsibility to care for a mother who only loved material and is now reaping the rewards of her ugliness by becoming alone and unhealthy. We left with the doctor proclaiming that we did not need another visit and were psychologically healthy, but needed to "completely" divorce ourselves from Jacquie, if we wanted to remain so!

Nicole enrolled in a medical transcription course and encouraged her cousins to gain computer skills so they can move into the future with more options for income production. She understands many of the ideas that her mother never attempted to even read and her training is preparing her for life away from me. She has complained that she does not want the responsibility of taking care of her mother once she has damaged her relationships with others, including siblings. Nicole may never be rich, but my wish is that she will know who she is, what she is about, and be true to herself.

She refused to get involved in her mothers scams and has told me that she made that decision in the mid eighties when she, Reggie and I returned from Los Angeles and found the police in our house, investigation one of her mother's staged burglaries. She explained that she was afraid that someone had actually been in her room and did not want to sleep alone until she, later, found all the things that her mother said were stolen, in the basement.

At one point she and her mother were in a car accident in which a guy scraped the drivers side of her Ford Escort. There was so little damage that she sold the car, without repairs, and at a very high cost, to a co worker's son, but her mother wanted to get money from the insurance company by claiming bodily injury. Nicole refused to play along, so her mother became angry. Jacquie then purchased a new Cadillac and later found another situation in which she made an unnecessary claim. Once again, Nicole refused to participate! I am proud that she internalized my standards!

I left good family, good friends and a sound community and moved, after military service, to San Francisco where I experienced a very different value system, but none of the craziness impacted my life until I met Jacquie. I realized, early in the marriage, that I had to make adjustments for the benefit of my children, as she spent most of the family resources on herself. To quote a family friend: "Jacquie is the most purely selfish person that I have ever known"! "Sandra, another of our associates, is selfish, but Sandra shares". "Jacquie shares with no one"!

One day I was telling Nicole how her mother's face changed during an argument. My daughter completed the idea saying: "To a demon, I have seen that face"! We then spent time talking about our feeling that there was always an evil presence in our living room, and agreeing that the presence is not as strong as it was when the entire family lived there. We continued that Jacquie seems to be uncomfortable in our home in Baltimore and on her last visits got really sick. She has a seeing eye dog and Nicole explained that the dog would go to the window in the room that we talked about and growl like a lion, when she first brought it home. When her mother would ask "Who is there" Nicole told her that no one was there! Later, The dog started hiding in the closet and when she pulled him out of the closet, the dog hid in the bathroom. The dog was very obedient, but avoided going back into the house once it got outdoors Jacquie complained that the dog became stubborn, unruly and walked her into walls. When she finally moved out of the house the dog changed back to being smart and protective.

Nicole and I attended a family reunion in Virginia, after which nineteen family members came to our smallish three bedroom home, in Baltimore. We used sleeping bags, the few beds that were available, air mattress, couches and the floor, but my daughter was in tears when the last family member left. I quickly realized that I had never seen her tears when in laws, and their children left following a visit. While everyone was in Baltimore I found myself wishing that Reggie was here, so I flew to San Francisco to get his daughters. When I returned, the little girls were smothered with hugs and kisses. My wife may have tolerated adults in her house in Denver, but it would have been to show that she has more than they have. She would never allow that many people in her much larger house, because someone would either break something, or steal from her and there was no way she would accept that many children. Only her siblings, or uppity friends have taken things from our home in the past.

Nicole and Reggie are the best thing that have happened in my life and I really feel sorry for men who give small amounts of time to their children. My memories of changing diapers and singing Johnny Mathis songs to Nicole when she had colic are precious memories I would take her into the living room, lay her on my chest, sing to her and enjoy the fact that she was my daughter. I had told myself that I didn't want children, because I saw so much abuse of during my years as a police officer, but realize that Nicole has been my reason to continue to move forward. When I talk of abuses I am not just speaking of physical, or verbal abuse, but improper rearing, failure to make decisions that benefit our offspring, failure to acquire necessary information to guide them and double standards, such as: "Do as I say, not as I do"! Yes, I "Spanked"! I set standards for myself and my children and never implied that my actions should be overlooked, because I was an adult. I lead by example and would not ask more of them than I asked of myself! I believe that a good parent is a mentor, leader and mentor.

Oldsmobile Advertises: "This ain't your father's Oldsmobile"! Well, these aren't your mother's, father's, or grandparent's children and this is not the 30's, 40's, or 50's. Words such as dumb, stupid and ignorant need to be replaced with concepts such as dyslexia and autism. And let us never forget the word "Dysfunctional", because parents who are content to pass aberrant behavior from generation to generation, without an effort to learn new ways, are doing more damage than drugs, alcohol, cigarettes, and all the racist on the planet. I listened to ugly music and discussed it. I watched my children, my children's friend's and my children's friend's parents, drew conclusions and developed solutions. My children were the most important issues in my life!

Chapter 4

My brother, Johnny, has said that I fell in love with Reggie and married Jacquie! When I first came into his life he was only three years old, so Johnny and I had a ton of fun with him. We would pick him up, tell him "Get off me" and toss him back and forth between the two of us just to hear him laugh. We took him to games when we coached, to karate practice, on field trips that we developed, for community residents, and practically everywhere we went. In the car we sang, yelled and screamed, because at her apartment Jacquie complained that we acted more like kids that Reggie.

The ladies on our female basketball team pampered him and rocked him to sleep, while the guys team played with him, teased and enjoyed his presence. Johnny and I were involved in many community activities and we took Reggie with us most of the time. Reggie was probably my reason for agreeing to try for a daughter, and my fondest memories are of my times with Reggie and Nicole.

One day, while we were working in our back yard, Jacquie was being so mean to Reggie that he drew his hand back and was going to punch her in the face. When he looked at me I gave him a look that implied that he would be in big trouble, if he did. I felt sorry for him, because she is the kind of person that wounds you then pours salt into the wounds. With both children her drama was "The intimidator", but she appeared to favor Reggie over Nicole.

Upon reading Nicole's term paper, I felt that I needed to talk to him, to get his input, but knew that he was never one to open up and express his feelings about his mother. Whatever I did with him was challenged by both his mother and grandmother, but I continued to do what I felt was right, hoping that he would know the difference. My college training suggested that I should be there when he reached out for support, but his reasoning was closer to hers than mine. When I punished him for not following house rules, his mother challenged decisions that I made, which created an impasse that I was unable able to bridge, until he became an adult.

I once told him that he could not live in the same house with me and stay out all night, with his friend, Jeff, at a young lady's house, while her parents were out of town, because I didn't want a male in the house with my daughter, when I wasn't home. I usually advised him, in the presence of his friends, so there was no confusion, but he and his mother suggested that I talked to his friends and never talked to him. Courtney, his best friend for many years, explained that I always talked when he and his friends were together, so Reggie and Jacquie became angry at Courtney. I talked to Jeff's father, and was naive to believe that he even considered the actions of his son as improper, but the possibility of a male at his house with his daughter while he was out of town was out of the question. Jeff's Father was as dingy as Jacquie on ethical issues, so I talked to Jeff's mother and found that she was as concerned about her son as I was about Reggie. She was also having difficulty talking to her husband.

Then there was always the debate between Jacquie and I about what Reggie wasn't doing in school and what he needed to learn to grow into a responsible adult. She taught him to drink beer and to drive fast, while I zeroed in on standards. She decided to teach him her concept of what a man should be, so he drove the car, when I told him not to and failed to do most things that I suggested would be beneficial to him. I was not surprised, but she got very upset, when she smelled marijuana on the phone following a conversation with one of his friends. "She taught him well"!

Jacquie and Granny did not seem to be concerned about what I taught Nicole, but challenged whatever I tried to instill in Reggie. Neither understood cause/effect relationships, so, they don't understand that they caused the turmoil that developed between Reggie, his ex wife, mother, grandmother and an aunt. Jacquie claims heredity against the father, so the misdemeanor of her sisters has nothing to do with the fact that her siblings do a poor job of parenting. Everything they do is self serving so children are nothing more than pawns: "The consequence of a weak moment"! Children are treated as dolls during infancy, but lose their status as humans once they grow beyond "Cute Toddler".

Reggie was sent to live with his natural father as soon as he turned eighteen and the decision was made without my consideration. I felt that he left before he was prepared to survive a world that was never going to meet him halfway. His dad and Granny provided a car, credit cards and living quarters, but he needed more. Granny always sent money, more clothes than he could wear and lots of toys, but was upset when I tried to teach values and discipline. Now he was going to live with her, his marijuana smoking, no respect for women, skirt chasing, dad and uncle. His Uncle Bud worked hard to change himself, but is the product of a social environment that one must leave behind, if he is to grow beyond it.

When Reggie moved back to California, Jacquie told all her friends that he was attending City College at San Francisco, but I overheard conversations from my old city college associates who confirmed that he was taking gym and health and following a pattern that had been developed early in his life. He was frustrated with school and not likely to work hard, which I attribute to his early years with his mother. If he mispronounced a word he was hit and she screamed and yelled, if he did not get concepts quickly. His first grade teacher, in San Leandro, California, did not like Blacks and the school district kept this secret until she retired the following year. He went from a demon in his first grade to an angel in his second year, so I had a conversation with the principal about the future impact of an irresponsible first grade teacher on a young impressive mind!

When I tried to help him study I noticed that his voice would rise and quiver and that he was easily frustrated. I attempted to explain that he should just relax and could see that he was really trying. As an adult, he stands up for himself and is quick to challenge those who take him for granted, but still needs to understand the value of an informed mind. I have seen him ask his mother to repeat statements, as if he can't believe what she just said, but she reiterates and he looks at her with disbelief. I know how he feels, because I had that feeling many times in twenty seven years. She has reason to be confident that what she is saying and doing makes sense, because she gets support from her sisters and other females who think like her, and she gets validated by our unethical system. I have training, skills and education, while she scams, lies, cheats and is rewarded for being ugly, selfish and devious. She got better jobs, and better pay, which would give anyone cause to believe that her, or she is correct in a belief system.

I suggested that she needs to stop creating false images about Reggie that will fall apart when he converses with informed friends and associates. I also tried to explained that his deficits, as a Black Male, were going to be different than for our daughter, and that his lack of effort was a prelude to future conflict. He didn't come to Denver for many years, so I decided that I would go to San Francisco and visit him. Each time I made the trip, Jacquie wanted to do other things. When his first child was born, I went to California attempting to see her, but Jacquie usually thwarted my plans. On one visit we all met at a restaurant and he hugged me as if I was a big teddy bear. My daughter told me that his first response, when he greeted her was "Where's my Dad"! He and I got a chance to talk, but I still did not get to see his daughter, until I decided to visit without his mother.

I flew out with my daughter and stayed in a hotel near the San Francisco Airport where he met us with, now, two daughters. I, also, got my first opportunity to meet the mother of his children. I listened and used my police training and sales skills to get answers that I needed. I had taken my daughter to my company's psychologist and, now, felt the need to know how Reggie was reacting to our dysfunctional marriage.

One year I sent him an airline ticket, so we could meet in Cancun, Mexico. When I got to the resort the people at the front desk let me know that he had arrived and that he was the life of the party. They told me a year earlier that I should be pleased, because my daughter exhibited more class than most Caucasians who come there, and now they were telling me how much they were enjoying Reggie. When I got near our rooms, there he was! All 270 pounds of him! With a glass of beer in each hand and a smile that charmed the workers at the resort from the time he got there until the day we left.

I took my son and daughter to Mexico many times during their childhood and knew they enjoyed Mazatlan and Puerto Vallarta, because there were no race issues to impede their fun. We traveled to Saint Thomas and Jamaica, but they had a unique attachment to Mexico, so we went often. Nicole had been to Cancun several times, but this was Reggie's first trip and he made the most of it. I left Cancun feeling that he was going to be okay, but told him that I would always be there when he needed a helping hand. Unfortunately, California has no equivalent to our brief stays in Mexico and he is finding that he has no support system with his mother, or father. My daughter and I have difficulty keeping contact with him, but I call regularly and leave message to let him know that I am still available, if he needs help.

My daughter has matured by leaps and bounds, since we moved east, but I am concerned that I need to do more for Reggie I told him numerous times that he always has a room and home in Baltimore, because I want him to feel welcome. I noticed that he has had an intellectual growth spurt, in recent years, is kind, friendly, socially aware and thoughtful. His reasoning skills are good and his smile still does wonders for those that he encounters. My next step is to try to talk him into going back to school. I know that I need to be very careful with this subject, but his ex girlfriend said that he wishes that he had continued his education.

His ex wife explained that he often refused calls from his mother. She said that she suggested that he call his mother, to which he would reply, "You don't know her"! She thanked us for visiting and explained that she always wondered if she would meet any of Reggie's Relatives and like them. She mentioned that her physic had told her that we would visit, and that Nicole and I were the first of her Reggie's family that she could even talk to. I was declared the official grandpa of the children and she and Nicole talked frequently for years until it became apparent that Reggie did no like her being an intermediary between he and us.

Reggie's mother is critical of individuals that she can't control, so his ex became a recipient of her venom. When I decided that I needed to talk to Reggie, I realized that I could probably get more information from his ex wife, so I asked questions and listened until I felt confident that I had answers to long unanswered questions. I wondered about the impact of his grandmother sending large sums of money to him when he was younger and felt that this impacted my efforts as a step dad, until it was suggested that his mom was keeping the money. I now knew that he, like Nicole and I, was a pawn and that we were all a part of a scheme to get what Jacquie wanted. I now understood why Reggie was always borrowing from Nicole, when his Granny sent him $200 and Nicole $20. Nicole was never one to spend money and complained when her shoe box with over $200 suddenly disappeared.

Granny told Reggie's ex that I showed favoritism and would feed him Cheerios, while cooking steaks for Nicole. Nicole loves Cheerios and was never much of a meat person, so when Reggie was asked, if what his

Granny said was true. His response was, "Don't pay any attention to her"! Granny never realized that she was also playing into Jacquie's scam, or that Reggie and Tanya might still be married, if there had been less interference from Granny, mom and Aunts.

Reggie is now with a young lady who loves him, but can not provide a support system. I decided that I need to do more and told him, again, that I will help in ways that I can. He commutes over 62 miles and his car over-heats, so I have suggested that he get an estimate for repairs which I will pay for. I am also working overtime to raise extra money for a computer, so he can stay in touch with his sister. His mother lives with her collection of material and got immoral support from her sisters and girlfriends until she was divorced and needed their help. She hasn't supported efforts to get Nicole through college, and I don't expect her to help Reggie.

Reggie and Katrina lived in a small world that includes themselves, her son, a new baby and infrequent visits from his two daughters, because Katrina feels that friends are messy and create turmoil. His dad, who fathered many children, has told him that he needs to stay close to him and Uncle Bud and not get caught up with "A woman"! I suggested that they might try a different environment, because there are places where family values are encouraged and friendship is important. His dad and uncle need his help to care for property that they own, while his mother wants to ensure that he inherits the property for her sake. He moved out of one of the houses, which is run down and so large that it would take half his salary to pay the utility bill. He has to make child support payments for his daughters, so he is heavily burdened and surrounded by individuals who don't understand that he could use some help.

I believe that one who is without spirituality is without a soul. My children are spiritual beings who neither lie, nor steal and have maintained the standards that I taught. They and are proof that heredity is not the only deciding factor as to whether one has ethical and moral values, but both have been impaired by the dysfunctional personalities that were been a part of their growing years. I feel that I owe both apologies and try to encourage them not to do as their parent have done, but to find ways to move beyond the world that they once perceived as shelter.

Nicole has done well once I removed her from an environment with relatives who are selfish and character flawed, but Reggie was born into a predicament that makes a similar adjustment much more difficult. He was thrust back into that predicament once he turned eighteen. The cousins that have encouraged a change in Nicole are viewed differently and her circle of friends is larger, because my side of the family sees all persons that we feel good about as family. My siblings children have always recognized Reggie as family and look forward to a reunion. His daughters have spent time with my brothers children and have felt the love and caring that was generated by my ancestors. We have asked Reggie's ex wife to visit with new found cousins in Los Angeles and we encouraged Reggie and Katrina to make the short trip. So far only Reggie's girl's have made the trip.

There is a paradigm into which Reggie can escape, and in which he will, hopefully, find greater fulfillment, but he needs to take the step. My brother, who lives in California, has extended his hand on more than one occasion, but Reggie has not yet reached out to grasp the possibility of a new beginning.

Chapter 5

By most standards we were considered poor, as we grew up in Roanoke, Virginia; but we always had things that money can't buy like: "Sound judgment, spirituality and grit"! I have always known that money can't buy happiness. Money is a tool for those who are grounded in reality, but a ticking bomb for those who are shallow of thought. Money can buy a big house, but cannot guarantee a sound foundation, or a good home. Money can buy pretty legs, full breasts, round hips and a great smile, but cannot guarantee love, fidelity, supportive habits, or a healthy outlook.

There are, in this world, rich fools, poor fools, young fools and old fools; an it is usually the case that an old fool was once a young fool. My psychology training implied that smart people get smarter and that those who are less capable become even more so. People can change, but money is not usually a factor. Being true to ones' self is the way to real happiness, and the only person that can make me happy is "Me"! When one is not sharing, caring and sensitive he will heap problems on others and never realize that he is a parasite, a blemish of nature that is of little value to humanity. Other humans should steer clear, and this type of person must realize that he will have no real friends, or realistic ties. It is difficult to compete against unethical efforts to gain material, girl friend nonsense, player mentality, electronic sex toys, support from siblings who encourage ugly habits and all the other B.S. that makes life difficult. I know! I have seen the signs of the succubus!

No matter how hard I tried to communicate, she never got the message and her excuse like many female's is: "We don't communicate"! It's true that we don't talk about real issues and that I keep quiet, rather than argue. I believe that I must leave a trail of good feelings behind me as I travel through life, so I am not taunted by the "ism's" that keep those with shallow minds at each other's throat. While I am not selfish enough to believe that I am the only right thinking person on the planet, I do try to get beyond the veil of nonsense that is layered across the minds of those who are willing to go along to get along at the expense of others who might offer insights into why we exist and what is necessary to become, spiritual, healthy, happy, functional and fulfilled.

After talking with my brother, sister, close friends and my company's EAP Psychoanalyst I now realize that I was the perfect tool. Like my brothers and sisters, my first concern is my children. I wanted them to have a mother and father in the home, so I remained in a relationship that close associates saw as meaningless. When the time was right, many who never offered a clue, found a way to tell me what they had been thinking for years! We had discussions about how long our marriage would last, and many were surprised that it took so many years for me to move on. My sister in law was anxious to tell me how she felt and admitted that she had waited eighteen years, while others, including my former tax accountant wasted no time letting me know just how they felt.

When I was young I felt invincible and had plenty of room for error, but as I got older it became important that I offer good information, values and traditions to my children, nieces and nephews. Being selfish, uninformed and misguided is a detriment to family and the future. Close friends expressed concern about the impact that my wife had on our daughter and her friend's self esteem. Many of her friends were without fathers and saw me as their strong male example. Some called me "Dad", which surprised students at her school, as so few of her friends were Black.

In sales we say "Luck is when preparation meets opportunity". This holds true in marriage and child rearing as in other life situations. We can't continue to bring children into the world and not prepare ourselves for the job of parenting. We are given these fantastic little beings to mold and develop and a large number of us are doing an incredibly poor job. Too much medication, too depressed and stressed, selfishness, greed, overindulgence and a lack of preparation are the real causes, but my ex blames her current predicament on the idea that Nicole and I are not there for her. She fails to understand that she was not there for us, was not willing to share with us, and is reaping what she has sewn and is sewing.

I sometimes feel that the system rewarded her for not improving, or polishing her skills, while I was punished for getting an education and trying to better myself. I set goals and expectations about what I needed to bring into a relationship and I took courses before I attempted to bring a child into this world. I have made mistakes, but I try to learn from each, because I don't like making the same mistakes over and over again! My Dad always said: "The only people that don't make mistakes are people that don't do anything"! I agree, but mistakes should not become habit! The impact of poor parenting shows up in our streets, prisons and mental wards across the nation. As a police officer , I saw the residuals as I worked with the San Quentin Squires and the California Youth Authority. I wanted to assure that my children did not become statistics in the criminal justice system, or social welfare system.

When I took my daughter to my company's psychologist, he told me that I needed to give her a home! We lived in three, not so nice apartments using second hand furniture and air mattresses until late 1997, but she actually seems happier. In Denver we lived in a very large well furnished house which Nicole and her close friends call the museum. She misses many of the items that were in the house, but says that Baltimore is her home city, because the people are family oriented and take time to teach their children. She is good at staying away from bad influences, but can also see good in people. I was reared around so many good people that I believed all people were good. She is far better prepared than I was at her age.

The downside is that she can be overly cynical. I have explained that cynicism can be good, but it can also become a crutch. I pray that she will learn control, but she is smart, intuitive and has a good heart. All I can do at this time is continue to be supportive and hope.

Chapter 6

I hear women blaming men for their actions, making statements like, "Women are just doing what men have always done", or "Women are just getting even for what men have done to them and "All men are dogs"! During these conversations, I usually remember how often I, or one of my friends have tried to warn female friends about a guy that we know is a jerk and how seldom they have taken our advice. These very same women blame all men when they feel used. The opposite is also true! The reality is that there are just as many sorry women as there are sorry men. Men are getting notoriety and it is about time for someone to talk about what women are doing, not doing, and getting away with! My ex is not that unusual!

There are guys who feel that women only care about a nice car, or money, so they lie about jobs, buy cars that they can't afford, or flash bankrolls at women that they want to impress. If you use gold as bait, you attract gold diggers, so why is the consequence a surprise? We send messages to our children that are of no value in helping them to develop standards, or the resilience that is necessary to survive this capitalist democracy. Wrong signals perpetuate disrespect, low self esteem, self hatred and weak communication skills that negatively impact the present and future.

Many of the complaints that I hear from women, I have experienced with women. I have had to back away from married and single women and I have known women that beat up boyfriends and husbands. I have been on stakeouts as a police officer and seen Prominent Black Females sneak out of hotel rooms with White Males, so I don't feel that there is much difference, when it comes to the issue of ethics and morality.

Many men refuse to think harshly of the mothers that have protected and cherished them, but treat other females like filth, because of things that they have seen their mothers do. Unethical females take advantage of stereotypes to get their way without realizing the damage that they do to sons and daughters. Some women tell daughters that all men are dogs, while in the presence of sons and the sons grow up referring to other women as bitches, because of disrespect that is initiated by mothers. We must be cautious with our words and nonsensical statements such as: "Do as I say, not as I do" are among the most ridiculous. We must lead by example! Any activity that is wrong for children, is wrong for adults and megalomaniacs who call themselves "players" usually have self esteem conflicts. Nothing is comparable to a serious monogamous relationship with a sensitive, caring partner who is willing to take time to learn how to please a significant other.

Happiness is an internal issue, so each of us is responsible for his, or her, own happiness. Any human being that thinks that he, or she gains by taking advantage of others, is a sick puppy and needs veterinarian treatment. Unfortunately, there aren't enough treatment centers and many of the worse offenders claim that they don't need treatment, and remain "Stuck on Stupid"!

When my wife suggested that she was going from Colorado to California to have lunch with a male friend she had met at her girlfriends birthday party, she got very angry when I suggested that she buy her own ticket and not use my passes. Her response was that I was trying to control her. I got the same response when I suggested that movies and dinner with male friends is not an appropriate habit for a married woman. She says: "I am against her having male friends and I am evil and chauvinistic"! Her sisters and some female friends reward her bad habits with the standard cliché: "You go girl", so when her friend's Husband suggested that her dating habits were inappropriate, and that he did not want her hanging around his wife, she sat on the stairs and cried, complaining that he was picking on her! She feels that a date is when you sleep with someone.

We are responsible for our actions once we move beyond our parents doors, and need to stop blaming what we do on some mythological being (the devil) that has no more power over us than we are willing to rationalize. We also need to learn the source of our craziness, grow up, get over it and stop blaming others for our lack of maturity. Guys that women call dogs usually have a lot of women and, if you hang out with dogs, expect to get bit, To the "Players" who are sleeping with all those "Bitches", a bitch is a female dog and I have a springer spaniel that is in heat, but I don't want her to have pups. Maybe after you she'll just forget that she needs a real dog. Once you make a mess of your life, don't blame your stupidity on the rest of us. Remember the song by Oscar Brown Jr. about a lady who picked up a half frozen snake, took it home, nursed it back to health and was surprised when it bit her. Knowing that she might die she pleaded that all she had done was try to be helpful. The closing lines of the song are: "Oh shut up silly women, said that reptile with a grin! "you knew damn well I was a snake before you brought me in!"

Black Women say: "Every time a Black Man makes it big he goes out and gets himself a White Woman." Well, Lena Horn, Dorothy Dandridge, Whoopie Goldberg, Flo Kennedy, Diana Ross, Della Reese, Alfre Woodard and one of my "favorite females" Maya Angelou, are a few of the Black Females who married White Men. The reality is that the majority of Blacks marry Black and too many of us spend too much time worrying about those who have made it big and too little time considering people that might be closer to us. We need to work to build relationships with people that are within our psychological and socioeconomic sphere and do a lot of soul searching.

Denzel Washington would be just an average nice guy, if he was not a big star and he appears to be very comfortable with a good wife and stable family! On the one occasion that I was able to shake his hand and get and get an autograph for Jacquie, he seemed open, honest, responsive and professional. Hoochies, groupies and most of the females that spend hours talking about how fine he is, are not in his league! If he ever met my ex I feel sure that he recognize her for what she really is" An unethical female, influenced by a succubus"! Women seem to pick up evil signals, but men see her as a possibility and move forward never noticing her claws and fangs.

"We need to get our value system and priorities straight". I love Maya Angelou for the image she projects and could care less about whom she happens to be married to. Alfre Woodard has big beautiful bedroom eyes, but all I can do is wish her good luck and hope that she is married to the man she loves. I had enough problems with the woman that I spent most of my adult years with: "Oh the lessons I was forced to learn"!

Chapter 7

As a young man I read everything that was available about male/female relations. There was Masters and Johnson, sexology and the school system put out sex education material titled Fathers and Son's, and Mothers and Daughter's. Information flourished and since I knew that I would never be some great looking hunk I read it all. I figured, if I ever met my dark-skinned beauty, I wanted to know how to satisfy her every need. I planned that I had to have completed at least two years of college and needed at least $700 dollars per month. My goal was $15,000 per year and I knew from watching all of the men around me that I should understand money and have a business plan for those times when I would endure unemployment. I had figured that Black Men had to make it by forty and have a nest egg, or there would be hard times ahead.

By eighteen I realized I that knew as much about the female anatomy as most women. I was naive about their motivations, but that really didn't matter, because I was only looking for one, and I was going to do everything I could to have her climbing walls. I would be patient and sensitive and learn, with her, the things that I would never do with anyone else. When she came down from the wall I was going to be waiting and there would have so much more that she would never want another man. If she wasn't completely satisfied, I would find out what I needed to do and fix the problem. I would write songs and poetry, learn how to tell her how precious she was; and there would be sweet, little names. My dad always called my mother "Honey Bunch"! I knew that I had to be in excellent physical condition, so I worked out regularly and was a better than average athlete, a six foot, slam dunking, forward and often ran five to seven miles a day.

I worked hard at any job I got and wanted to eventually become a businessman, because one thing was obvious: "Education was not getting Black Men the kind of freedom I wanted"! The best example I knew of a free Black Man, during my early years, was A.G. Gaston who practically financed the Selma, Alabama, Civil Rights March.

My first girlfriend was Patricia and she was so pretty that I never understood why she chose me. I was poor, skinny, nothing to look at and seldom went to school, because I didn't have the clothes and was always hungry. Our first kiss put me into a state of bliss that I didn't understand, but I felt that I must have looked completely silly as I left her front porch. I went into the Air force to find a better life, and when I got to England she sent me the words to Etta James new recording. In her letter she wrote: "When I heard you were leaving, All I could do was cry"! I also started getting letters from others girls, but knew that young girls like to write guys who went away to the military. Before I left home I heard that Patricia liked someone else, but I never asked, because I never understood why she liked me anyway.

Though I only made it through the ninth grade, I took the GED and college courses in the Air Force, and was doing well at City College at San Francisco, when I met and fell for a petite, dark-skinned beauty named Angie. Things were going well until one of my friends told me that I was sleeping in another mans bed and eating his food. He had seen my car outside the apartment and presumed that I did not know that she lived with another man. He advised me that she was getting married a few weeks later, and that the reason that I had not run into him was that he was on the road selling encyclopedias.

Angie was my dream girl: a nurse who knew what she was about. She danced for me wearing only the top of a short nightie and those firm round hips would make me crazy. She had this way of frowning and complaining that I didn't want to make love to her, was cute, slick and knew what she wanted in a man. I thought that I knew what I wanted in a woman, but obviously didn't know what I needed in a woman. She closed her legs when we made love and explained that she needed clitoral stimulation. "That wasn't in the books that I read!" She had me and a fiancee, and when I approached her about this little triangle, she didn't lie.

She explained that I was strong and she loved me, but she needed to marry a man that she could take care of and asked me to come to her wedding. At the wedding she asked: "If we could still be lovers" and suggested that, if we couldn't, she had a girlfriend. I was not happy that I had been in another mans apartment, because some have been killed for less and I wasn't going to college to be stupid. I admire her for knowing what she needed and for what I learned from her, but quickly realized that I wanted to go in a different direction. Angie was ahead of her time and was the first at City College to wear a natural hair style. I was visiting a friend that I had met through my sister, when she removed a scarf and revealed her new style. The guys went into to the next room and laughed, never knowing that this was to be the insignia of the revolution in the late sixties and early seventies.

I thought I had my life all mapped out and was well on my way to meeting my goals. During the confusion, I met Estelle who always sat on the same stairs, and was always studying. Estelle had a lovely smile and big beautiful eyes, so I called her "Star Eyes", and sang Johnny Mathis' "Stella by Starlight", or Sarah Vaughn's rendition of "Star Eyes" to her. Her favorite song was "Don't mess with Bill"! We talked, about inconsequential things, but she was pleasant, polite and classy. She didn't hang around the lounge, or cafeteria, but saw Angie and I together, and sensed that something was wrong. She went to Angie's wedding with me and we sat there, confused, but her understanding was such that I left without suffering a panic attack. We gave Angie credit that she was not confusion about what she wanted, and Estelle teased me about the relationship, because she knew my moral standards. I was young, naive and learning, so Angie gave me a sociology lesson and Estelle taught me about love"!

She was warm, sweet, sincere, kind hearted and loving and to this day I miss the love I could see in her eyes. The down side was that I could also see her pain and I never adjusted to that after I filed for the divorce: "The biggest mistake of my life". We had fun together and my family loved her much as I did. I will never forget her running through the airport toward me when she came back from trips visiting her grandmother, who lived in Louisiana. We partied, traveled, danced, made love and "Were friends"! Our relationship was a natural follow through from my life as a child and there were times when we awaken in the middle of the night with so much passion that we never realized that we were in the midst of a hot love making session until it was too late to stop. I had a playboy key, she was my playmate and we were into each other. My time with her was the most loving experience that I have known as an adult. I know Estelle loved me and "I feel stupid", because I left a woman that was willing to give me that much love. I read the books, but "I wasn't ready"!

Her sister Vanessa became my little sister. I took her to get her hair done, gave gifts when she did well in school and encouraged her to grow to her potential. She was a kind sweet child and loved her big sister in the same way that I love and respect my eldest sister, Yvonne. Her mother and the friends that came with Estelle were loving and caring, so I found my paradise, but was too young, to hurried and too unaware to stop and realize what I had.

I think about a day when I was stretched out on the couch during a brief earthquake and she jumped, seemingly, across the room and landed on me, because she was frightened. I was pleased that in a moment of distress she came to me, rather than move. I worked lots of hours during our days together, but our time together was ours. We enjoyed the same friends, our relatives were close, and people that I met through her understood, and were sensitive to our needs.

I remember my first Christmas with her family and friends. I received very few gifts as a child, but was proud, if I only got a pair of my fathers socks, because: "He was my dad"! Anne, one of the family friends purchased this sweater for me and I must gotten had a strange look on my face, because she came over, hugged me and asked, " Honey, you are not accustomed to getting gifts, are You"! I wondered how she knew and why did she and her husband, George, let me to drive their brand new Chrysler New Yorker. How could they like me so much that they let me drive their brand new car? "That is not the California Way"! I knew guys who wouldn't let their wives drive their car and in Cali, "Material is not everything, it is the only thing"!

In 1967 we purchased a brand new Chevrolet Caprice, and Estelle was driving from a parking meter, in the Mission District. A truck hit the drivers side of the car and tore out drivers side front and rear windows, so she called me and was so upset that she had parked the car in the garage, at our home, until she could explain what had happened. She kept apologizing, while I kept asking if she was hurt, trying to explain that the car was not as important and that we had insurance. She was concerned about the car, but I could always buy another car: There was only one Estelle. We never had financial problems, because we worked together and we didn't keep secrets from each other She never embarrassed me in public, and always left a trail of good behind her, we were comfortable in all settings, and she was love, so nothing was more important than she.

At the beginning of our marriage we moved into an apartment next door to Al Jarreau and his wife Phyllis, who always reminded me of a "White" Barbara McNair. I couldn't understand why Al was always talking about these hot looking Black women that he had seen at the Half Note

Club, while he was married to Phyllis. We would stand out on the balcony away from our wives to go through little chats. At times Estelle would come outside and I would look at her and look at Phyllis, who always had a cigarette in her hand and realize that of the two women I really had the prize: "She was like and angel in disguise". I had not yet become immersed in the activities that would eventually separate us, so I was content to spend my evenings and weekends with her.

I became involved in politics, community projects and travel, while still in college and most of what I did I wanted her to be with me. I never realized that she couldn't possibly have my energy level, since nobody else did. I was disappointed that she couldn't understand my need to run a business and, since I was working 16 plus hour days I couldn't understand why she wasn't doing more to help. The truth was that I had set my goals too low, was confused, on a collision course to burnout and breakdown and had no real idea what my next move should be. She was what I wanted and needed, but I was moving too fast to understand. I thank God for the years we spent together, because they were my best. She taught me to love in a way that I hope I have taught my son and daughter.

The beginning of the end started when I was moved from patrol duty to the community relations unit. I became involved in so much that I lost one of the most fantastic women that God ever gave breath to. I had a karate club, a male and female basketball league, took children on educational tours, showed full length movies in the schools, helped in developing the first swimming pool for the neighborhood, worked closely with the five most committed ladies in the community, went to court with community residents when I felt that they were being treated unfairly and participated in so many activities that during the holidays I would get twenty four hour flu. One day I hurt my knee, but kept on working, even after the fluid was drained. I was too busy to pick get prescribed medication, so when Estelle got home I was on the floor, holding my knee, and in tears.

I was driven to participate, so I neglected my wife, and when I thought that I was driving her crazy, I filed for a divorce. When I filed for the divorce it seemed that every woman on the planet knew about it and even the wife of an employee wife asked me to bed with her. On one occasion I was taking one of the community workers to a business lunch and she suggested that we go straight to a motel. I got so many offers that I was really afraid to let anyone know that I was not married.

The last time I saw Estelle was at a party next door to her mothers home. I was with Jacquie and she was with a date. When I saw the pain in her eyes, I vowed that I would never do to another woman what I did to her. For many years I thought that I was paying for the pain that I caused her and when she died at the age of thirty five, some of my old friends told me that I broke her heart. Still, she gives me the strength to go on. I carried a lot of guilt for eleven years, but I now know that "God put us together and we will be together"! Estelle's essence was burned into my soul and she remains, and will always be a part of me. She was an Angel and life with her was heaven. Life with Jacquie was a tour of the other place, but my years Estelle gave me strength to survive, the insight to look back, correct my efforts and build a better life. Reggie and Nicole were reasons to continue, but Estelle's essence was my guide. The children kept me moving forward and Estelle keeps me strong!

I made the mistake of divorcing Estelle before maturing and understanding her love for me. I was busy fighting every cause as an activist, but failed to take on the cause that made me complete. When she died I carried the guilt of knowing that I broke her heart, vowed to never make that same mistake and never to treat another human being that way, so many of the mistakes with my second wife were the byproduct an all consuming guilt. Our divorce was my undoing and after driving past her home many times, for many years, I finally went in and apologized to her mother. She explained that Estelle said on her dying bed "Mamma I may have been wrong, but I loved him"! Her mother then asked: "What about that boy"!

My brother says it was Reggie that I fell in love with and that he knew that I would stay married until the children were grown.

Estelle's mother asked, if I was stuck on myself and maybe that is why I divorced her daughter. I explained that I didn't know who I was during those years and was involved in too many things to stop and find out. I suggested that I knew better in later years, than when I was married, how much Estelle meant to me, because it is her essence that has given me the strength to continue pressing forward.

I always thought that I was the black sheep of my family and needed to live up to someone else's ideals of who I should be, until I started talking to my brothers and sisters, and realized we all thought we were black sheep. My parent's always showed love and caring and I was fortunate to have been around when they were together, so I had the benefit of knowing that both wanting me to want to do well, but I really didn't know what doing well meant. It was my time with Estelle that helped me to become the man that I am today and to realize that I am okay. I was okay then, but didn't know it. The love of family is very important and special, but nothing compares to the love I found in her. Hopefully, I have paid for my mistakes and deserving of a better future.

In 1987 I purchased a 1984 Black Chrysler that had 57,000 miles on the odometer, and had over 224,000 miles in 2000, when I gave it to the Salvation Army. I called the car "Beauty" and told people: "There is an angel in my car" and that angel encourages me to not lose my spirit. My daughter feels that she knows Estelle, and feels her presence, and loves the car, but Jacquie hated it from the day I first saw it and talked to the lady minister who sold it to me. At were times when I might have become depressed, while driving home on the freeway, I sensed that Estelle was in the back seat urging me to carry on. I have turned, or looked into the rear view mirror and not seen her, but I know she was there. She is always there! While married we did everything together and talked and compromised about what we did. I feel that we are still together and she is still helping me to make good choices. I, sometimes, slip up in favor of my daughter, but she understands: "I know she does"!

Chapter 8

There was one woman that I have to give credit for being, not just a smooth operator, but also the best sex partner I have ever been with. She was smart, aggressive and read me like a book, and it was she who actually helped me to get on with my life. I was getting barraged by women and I couldn't understand why. Charlene read me immediately, knew my dilemma and cornered me in a way that no woman has been able to do so since. She taught me that love is more than sex, and that good sex is always better with someone you love. If you are lucky enough to be in love with one who cares enough to go that extra yard to please you, count your blessings and reciprocate, because things could be worse. Once you mess up a good thing, there is no guarantee that your next significant other will be an improvement. Often what appears to be good is only temporary. Trust me, I found out the hard way!

I met Charlene as just another community project, while doing things that I became accustomed to doing. I visited her in the hospital, met her mother and two children and loaned her a small TV for entertainment.

One night, after she came home, she told me that she needed to get away from all the noise and asked me to drop her off at a motel. Not thinking, I played right into her hands! When I got to the motel she asked me to just sit and talk to her for a few minutes. She said that she wanted to thank me for all that I had done for her, but was so smooth that I spent the night at the motel. She had this saying "I can do more with a penis than a monkey with peanuts", and she was right. Like Angie, she knew her strengths and had me mesmerized. When she found out that my brother was staying with me she got one of her friends to run interference. Angie was cute and slick, but Charlene was a master, a connoisseur. She understood me so well that it took major effort to move away from her and I still have visions of sweet lovemaking sessions. The last night I spent with her was in Reno and she made that night a night that I will always remember. I drove she and her mother there, supposedly, to see a show, but we spent the night in bed. We made love so much that I would get blisters from the friction, but she made it worthwhile, and she knew it. She had the good judgment to know that most women don't understand a men anymore than men understand women, so she had the option to choose the man she wanted. I feel lucky that she chose me.

When I told her that I needed more than just great sex, she looked at me and said "I love you, and I know how to make love to you: "You will remember that"! She was right: "I still remember"! "She was the best", and it was she who convinced me that men and women are trying to resolve similar issues while searching for love. Sex is not necessarily love, but sex is special, when you love the person that you are with. She must have read the books that I read and understood them better than I. She took the time to do things to satisfy me, but I was not in love with her. Jacquie should be very thankful to her, because I would have been sleeping with other women during those years that I was getting kicked out of bed, if I had never met Charlene. Estelle set me on the right course about love, but Charlene completed my training and taught me to be selective. I have spent the years after her trying to be as good to my woman as Charlene was for me. When I thought about having a loving, caring women, on the side, during my years with Jacquie, I decided against it.

Later, in the relationship, found that Charlene was married to a guy who was stationed with the Air Force in Amsterdam. I will always have good feelings about her, because she taught me one of life's great lesson. I have always been one to move to a higher plane once I learn, so when women approached me as some women say they are approached by men, I know that most stories about good loving are myths! There were women before Charlene that I now view from a different perspective, and Jacquie, more than anyone, benefitted from my having known her.

To most of the woman that I have known, I owe a pleasant "thank you", but there were also those who saw me as a walking penis and Charlene helped me to recognize the difference. Some wanted closeness and respect while fulfilling a physical need, while others were only concerned that their sexual needs were met. Jacquie is in the latter group, but I gave her what Charlene gave me and added the love that I learned from Estelle. In return I got about sixty percent of Reggie and ninety five percent of Nicole!

Margaret, a British girl, picked me out of a crowd of and treated me so well that I could have married her, but wasn't willing to go through the racial taunting that was 1960's U.S.A.. Women in Europe proved far more open minded than women in the U.S. I remember the competition at the Airmen's Club and how Margaret stood up and said to another G.I. "I am going to spend some time with him", while pointing at me. When she was with me there were no cigarettes, or alcohol, but lots of communication and lovemaking. She was warm and caring and good, but I was not ready to settle down. I remember how often girls, who visited the base would tell me whom they would marry, before they were involved with a particular guy, and how often they were right. Margaret may have had that discussion and I enjoyed my time with her, but I was on a mission to grow beyond my beginnings. I spent my early years in housing projects, rundown houses, and an orphanage, so I knew what it was like to do without and wanted to assure that neither I, or my children repeated such experiences.

I always had a couple of chickens and plenty of fries and drink for lady friends who visited the base, because I knew from whence they came. The consequence was that, whether I went to London, Leicester, or Peterborough, I always had a place to sleep. I treated women the way I wanted to be treated and they responded with kindness and caring. Margaret was a good woman, and took me to my first climax, but the timing was wrong. I had far to go, much to learn and met her in the sixties, before interracial dating was accepted in the U.S. of A. To have brought her to the states would have been grossly unfair to both of us.

Eve, a georgous Young San Franciscan, put her bed in a closet, so she could use the walls for amorous positions. I met her in a Laundromat and remember the night she asked me: "Bill, if you wanted to do something and knew that no one would get hurt, would you do it"? I said yes, even as I had no idea what she meant, but quickly found out! We would not see each other for months and it would seem like we had never missed a day, because we would start again where we left off at our last meeting. She moved one block from The Divisadero, when I walked the beat, so we spent my lunch hour in passionate lovemaking sessions. I thought it was the uniform, but wish I knew then what I know now. If I lived in the Bay Area we could always be friends, because she was special, and she was beautiful. "Why was I was lucky enough to be with her"? The last time I saw her she had married a Jewish Guy and I wondered whether he had the good judgment to appreciate her more than I. I still wonder if I will ever see her again.

Bernadette simply wanted a friend. She would have been satisfied, if we played tennis, or went to an occasional movie, but I was too busy. She was an excellent athlete, but not confident about her looks. She had perfect legs and a lovely dark chocolate complexion. A warm caress and a nibble behind her ears and she was ready. There have been times when I have longed for more of that unbridled passion, and wondered how I got my way with no strings attached. Other women acted as if they were some-thing extraordinary, but Bernadette was a sweetheart who appreciated the little time that we spent together. Had I not had been so involved in so many things, maybe I could have learned to really appreciated her, but the time was not right. She was a good woman who deserved more than I offered, but took the little that I gave and moved on without so much as a whimper.

I should have been smart enough to spend more time with her, but, I had meetings and rallies to attend, programs to administer, field trips to monitor, teams to coach,…. I was so caught up in helping everybody that I spent too little time with some good women, so I felt that I had no right to complain about settling with a Jezebel. Maybe I will met Bernadette again on one of my visits to San Francisco. We will have conversation about who I was then, who I am now and become true friends. I would love an opportunity to thank her for adding to my life, and would take care to be honorable and sensitive, because that is what she deserves.

The lady that I will always remember and cherish memories of is Alice Tribble, the daughter of a Mississippi Preacher. We never made love, because she was too young at eighteen, while I was twenty. I saw her, through her older sister Virgie, as one of God's Special Editions and vowed that I would not violate her. She was willing to go as far as I wanted, but I wanted to remember her as I first met her. I couldn't understand what she saw in me, when she could have chosen someone who looked as good as she. Her brother in law asked me not to get her pregnant, so I explained that I had watched his wife and was so impressed with her that I would never hurt Alice who was as beautiful and graceful as a swan. I always wonder where she is and how she is doing. I hope that I left a good impression, because she deserved the best. It has been my experience that not making love, like too little foreplay, leaves some women with a bad taste about relationships. Many fail to understand a male's reasoning about sex, so not being aggressive has proved to be as negative as being too aggressive with some women.

Let me explain: When I met Alice I had just broken up with Joyce, a Panamanian Lady, whose favorite statement was "Let's go motel"! She was so hot that, when I visited my sister in San Francisco, she would follow me into the bathroom, and that was embarrassing. I was her sweety, so when I heard guys lie about dating Joyce, while we were at Travis Air Force Base, I knew better, because she was always with me. After games we made love in the car and when there was no game she wanted to make love wherever we happened to be. She was sweet, but she smothered me and I wasn't ready for that much attention. We fogged up many a car window and wrinkled as many motel sheets. She had the energy of an athlete, because she ran track, and I was in tip top condition playing base level basketball. She was always ready and her "Darling" her "Sweety" had to be ready to!

The girl that I dated after Alice was a "Church Girl", but dumped me because, in her own words, "I was not aggressive enough"! She taught me about rejection. I was hurt at the time, but my pain turned to anger, because, in my mind, I was being the good guy. When she explained that she wanted to be with one of the guys from my squadron, I felt betrayed. I try never to disrespect women and, admittedly, could have done a better job of understanding her needs. Because of my upbringing, women have chosen to be with me, except in the instance of Estelle, Alice and my current wife Edita: "We each chose the other".

Fran was interested in a young, virile sex partner. She would call and say that she was horny and expect me to drop by and satisfy her needs. She was a thirty five year old Portuguese lady and had a boyfriend who was an entertainer performing in Reno and Las Vegas. I was twenty two and met her at a party, in our house that was filled with college students. I decided to go to bed and went to my room. There were three bedrooms, a kitchen and a bathroom on our floor and we all slept in rooms with doors that locked from the outside. She came to my room and climbed into bed. She then put on call for whenever she needed loving. Her apartment was between my job at the post office and my apartment, so she would call and ask me to stop by and treat her on my way home. She was mature and vocal about how she wanted to be loved and said that she wanted no additional attachments, but told me that she would cut off my testicles, if she caught me making love to her roommate, who was closer to my age. I was always leery of women who threatened me with bodily harm, so I moved on. When I was younger a girl that I had no ties to, cut my wrist telling me that she did not want to catch me with another girl, and I never forgot that encounter!

Other women were so into themselves that I moved away quickly. One young lady, who worked with the FBI, found out where I lived and left notes under my door until she convinced me to stay overnight at her apartment. I met her when I was on tour of San Francisco's FBI Office during training at the police academy. She bragged that I was lucky to have slept pent in her bed and introduced me to, her idea of, successful men who wanted to marry her. When I failed to play her game she refurnished her apartment and went home to Houston, Texas to retrieve a guy that ultimately married her: "All this to prove, to me, that she was something special"! I can't even remember her name!

A teenager who was as developed as a grown woman found out where I lived and stalked me for months. I knew she was too young because I met her in a California Youth Authority Cottage, so between this young lady and the FBI Agent, I learned to be private about where I live. Other women were so obvious that a first meeting emitted warning signals, so I moved away quickly. Some thought that they were so fine that in light petting sessions I heard words like: "Why are you breathing so hard"! I was not god's gift, but I liked myself more than that. I was an excellent athlete, in college, and far from "Stupid".

In telephone conversations women would say: "Bring your meat", when you come over tonight and job associates that I would go to lunch with would suggest that we go straight to a motel. An employee's wife, when I was President of The Bayview Hunters Point College, came right out and asked me to sleep with her. When I suggested that it was not a good idea, she came to my office, one night when I was working alone, locked all the doors, went into my conference room, disrobed, lay on the conference table with her goodies aimed at my door and called me. Another young lady refused to wear a coat over her close fitting dresses, when we went out on a date and told me that she wanted to "Live fast, die young and have a fine corpse"! Until that date, I had really thought that I had a crush on her.

As a police officer I heard statements like: "If you arrest me, I will put some of this good stuff on you and you will be glad to let me go"! Women have short, convenient memories and tell stories that are different from the way things really happen. There were those who would tell me, at the beginning of a conversation, that all they wanted was sex, so I thought they might have a disease and moved away. I think back to when one of my friend's father told me how hard it would become to get women into bed when I became and adult but learned that women aren't really so different. They are just as quick to approach men and some make it known that sex is what they want. Women dare men, just as men dare women, but women develop strange memories once they get sexed and place all of the blame on men. Some want sex and love, but act as if the sex is because of something the male has done wrong.

Most of the women that I became intimate with gave me something to admire and, with the exception of Jacquie, I have been lucky enough to steer clear of women with no standards. I always felt that I needed to learn something new, every day of my life, and what can be more daring than learning about women from women. Men and women are different, while having common interests and needs, but we are confused about what we need versus what we want, and do a great job of getting reality and illusion reversed.

Women who met Jacquie often asked me out, saying that they could see that she was about money and probably not so good as a wife. My approach was to always be respectful when I said no but some would tell male friends that I was "Whipped", laugh and say that I might accept their flirting, but would not go the extra yard. I always explained that accepting their flirting was a way of learning all the nice things I wanted to say to my special lady. I flirted with Estelle throughout our marriage and she always responded positively, but Jacquie responded negatively to everything I said, or did.

Chapter 9

I always wanted a lot out of life, but more than anything else I wanted respect and that was too much to ask for; "In her house"! I had to tolerate bad manners, lying, profanity, the light-weight criminal mentality, constant complaining and all of the ugliness that makes us, as a nation, one massive group of underclass citizens. We all pay for insurance fraud, shoplifting, and credit card scams, but we merely watch and hope that some power greater will intervene and stop the craziness. Meanwhile, our values decay, women are angry at men, most ethnic groups are angry at Whites who are in positions of power, children are angry at parents, the rich get richer, the powerful get more powerful, the bleeding continues and "The beat goes on"!

Frederick Douglass, once said "Until all men are free, no man is free!" As he was one of my heroes, during my early years, as were Nat Turner, Harriet Tubman, Sojourner Truth, Denmark Vesey, and others, I quote him a lot. "Judge not the Black Man by the heights he obtains, but by the depths from which he came" is another of my favorite quotes. I realize that with freedom comes a finite responsibility and that the depths that I have had to climb from were enhanced by selfish Black Males and Females and go along to get along jack asses who have no vision of the damage that they inflict on me, my children, my community, or those who come after us. Employment discrimination, racism, sexism and most of the ills of this nation are perpetuated by a selfish few who want control and don't give a damn about others. Control fanatics ruin politics, neighborhoods, churches, families and everything they have contact with. I saw it in individuals when I was a police officer, on athletic teams and when I was just having fun with friends. I once had to stop one of my best friends from squeezing my four year old son between his legs and asking "Do you give"!

There can be no real freedom until we begin to recognize that controllers are male, female, Black, White and other! They are individuals whose only concern is self. Fools get involved with these controllers seeking power that they will never achieve and like links in a chain, provide protection and support for those who could care less whether others fail, or succeed, survive, or starve, live or die. Controllers are everywhere and many of us know what they stand for, but feel that we will be okay, if we can just get our little edge of the proverbial pie.

The real solutions: "Cut the B.S", challenge mind games, move to a higher spiritual level, meet good people, support families and friends and let fools play fools games! But, "We must fight back"! If we don't challenge those who make our existence miserable, things will not improve.

In 1968 I was given the task of developing a community education project that was later called The Bayview Hunters Point Community College. I couldn't understand why I was chosen, because I had not finished my degree program at San Francisco State and wanted to go on to law school at SMU in Dallas, Texas. I was giving a presentation at one of the neighborhood child care centers and saw Jacquie as just another of those California Mothers who pampered her boy, dressed him like a doll and put him on exhibit. A friend had asked the school to have me speak, at the school because she knew that I was working with children at San

Francisco State's Child Study Center and felt that I had interesting things to say to the mothers at the school. I was trying to understand how so many parents did such a poor job of rearing children, so I hired a child development specialist to teach and help me develop a curriculum for the college.

I had seen some of the worst parenting imaginable, and felt that it was my job to do something about it, so I took as many child development courses as I could fit into my major. I wanted to make a difference and, for sure, I wanted to do a better job, if I ever became a parent. I did not want to add to the numbers of confused, dysfunctional children that I had to deal with as a police officer and in most instances that I encountered problem children, I knew why they had problems once I met the parents.

The friend who invited to speak at the school was different. She had three children, but never used them as a crutch. I later, saw an article in Ebony Magazine where she had finished college and gotten a big position at IBM. Jacquie used to tell me "If I hadn't got you, she would have". I had known Carolyn for some time and while she was very attractive there was no chemistry. Carolyn knew her responsibility and made no excuses for having to raise three children alone. I hoped that as a father I would be as good and not make the lame excuses that I heard from some women. Many of the mothers were good, but others were full of excuses, short-sighted, selfish, incapable of controlling themselves and blamed men that they "CHOSE" to sleep with! The best years of my life were those spent rearing my children, and it was neither too difficult, nor too time consuming. I tried to teach my children that spiritually is more important than money. Usually a person who is unhappy without money is unhappy with money. A poor jerk will probably be a rich jerk, if he acquires wealth!

The second time I saw Jacquie was on a nice day in April 1971 and she was walking home from her girlfriends house. I notice that she had a really fantastic smile, so we talked briefly until she asked me to come by and meet her son. She mentioned a couple of habits that I might be able to help her break, so I agreed. As we sat talking, in her apartment, I felt that

I had known her all my life. I didn't understand the connection, because I was still thinking that most people want to do the right thing. Over the years I came to realize that she always had a hidden agenda. I now feel that she came into my life, so I can learn that all that glitters is not gold. Until I met her I thought that all humans were basically good and spent time with the San Quentin Squires trying to bring out good that I did not find in some inmates.

I remember talking to my next door neighbor, who drove the Third Street Bus, and he implied that she was hot and easy, but I had no prurient interests, so his statements didn't concern me. I did try to explain to her that she needed to change her profile, with men, because images and innuendoes destroy your reputation, even when you are doing nothing wrong.

There was this old guy, "Nick", who ran a service station on Third and Palou, and gave her money. Then, there was this other woman who suggested that she must have been giving it up, or Nick wouldn't be giving her money. I felt that I had done all that I could to warn her, but later in our marriage, I realized that she knew what she was doing and never cared to heed my warnings.

I was glad to spend some time with her, because I was beginning to feel like a piece of meat, and she was gorgeous. She had this beautiful dark chocolate complexion, a great smile, and a perfect butt. As we became sexually active I began to feel that this was the woman that I had spent all those days studying for. I found that we did sexual things that I could never do with another woman, and I can still remember how she shuddered the first time I ran my tongue across her inner thighs, down her back, or across her waist. I wasn't sure just how to actually do some of the things that I had read about, but I figured that I would practice, on her, until I got it right. My relationship with Estelle was very proper and upright, so the things that Jacquie and I did were off-limits in my marriage to Estelle. My ego would hit the ceiling when Jacquie would ask, if I was going to treat her again.

Later when she would give me that look and ask, if I was going to do her, I would get the feeling that I was really on target.

In 1972 we took our first trip to Mazatlan Mexico and had so much fun that I just knew that we were going to be together forever. We had been having so much good sex that sometimes she often didn't make it to work on time the next morning. I still had a playboy key, so we went out and danced, went on picnics and made life all that I had dreamed it could be. I really felt that I had found my soul mate and she had a three year old son, so I actually got a ready made family. I had seen so many kids abused that I had already decided that I didn't want to bring any children into the world, but she changed all that, and told me that she wanted a girl.

Reggie and Nicole were the highlights of our relationship and to this day I have her to thank for that, but I now know, if I had slowed down, and if Estelle and I had been lucky enough to have a child, would we have stayed together. She would have been a fantastic mother and who knows, I might have grown up and made adjustments that were necessary. Reggie was a real plus in the relationship, but Nicole was the tie that bound us together.

Jacquie was a controller who cared only about herself and left behind a trail of bad feelings, but wonders why she has no long term friends"! Men are not always the culprit and women are not always the victim. I married a woman that was warm, kind and loving during our first two years together, but within the month after we took our vows the other woman reared her ugly head. If she wanted material gain, she should have gone to school, trained herself and worked toward her goals. We could have developed a game plan that would have been beneficial to the entire family; instead, the family became tools, so her high maintenance, low profile stature created a gap in all efforts to become a team: " A family"!

Like many misguided females, she is quick to say that she knows that she has class which she equates with her furs, her jewelry, her house, cars and job. She had all this, while the rest of the family was to keep the furnace turned down low, so the heating bill was less costly. I wore work uniforms as often as possible, had shoes resoled and wore clothes that were ten to fifteen years old to save money, while she spent money that we didn't have. Her most common complaint is: " We don't communicate", so the more I talked, the less she listened. The real problem is that she had a hidden agenda and used our marriage as a blank check to perpetrate fraud.

My move west exposed me to shallow women with misplaced values who believed that they could become happy by accumulating material. They equate material and class, so friends and family become tools. "Thank God for good family, quality friends and Estelle! My time spent with Estelle gave me the strength to survive Jacquie's craziness. I now realize that the good that was Estelle caused me to challenge the ugly that was Jacquie.

When I left Denver, she did the unethical things that she could not do when we were together. I maintained my integrity and stayed close enough to observe while offering her the chance to build upon what we started. Then she crossed the line and talked her father into trying to convince me to help in an insurance scam: "It was time to move on"!

Months later, when I was told that she was seen coming out of Reggie's Dad's bedroom in sleep wear, during the time we were married, I shut the door on any possibility that we would ever be together again. It took many years for Reggie's ex wife to tell me. She explained that she did not know me at the time, and that Reggie told her to "Leave it alone!" After talking to our insurance agent I found that Reggie also knew that she was going to file the false insurance claim that was to be the final straw. He never refuses his mother, as is common with most boys!

Chapter 10

It was a nice April day and Jacquie had come straight from work to Baltimore. As usual she wanted to go to TJ MAXX before settling in at the apartment. I hadn't purchased any furniture and slept on the floor, or an air mattress for two years, because I sent every spare penny to help with her EEO Litigation. I, even gave my guest passes from the airline that I worked for to the lawyer to encourage him to do as much as was practical. I was comfortable doing whatever was necessary to make her brief stay pleasant. I had been told by my daughter and a family friend that they suspected that she was shoplifting, while I lived in Denver, so I usually waiting in the car when she went shopping. I was not going to jail for something that she might do.

She takes advantage of whomever she comes into contact with and will not live in Baltimore, because retail employees see through her games. When they outsmarted her she called them evil bitches until she was arrested. She decided that she did not want to live in Baltimore, which was a good decision, because she needs to live in an area where agencies and employees are unskilled. One of her best friends refused to listen when I told her how selfish Jacquie was, but learned the hard way, when Jacquie borrowed a set of outdoor chairs and table for a lawn party, then told her that they were stolen when she wanted them returned. She suggested that she put them at the front of our house and came back to find them gone. The lawn set never left the basement and it didn't matter that she already had two sets of the same lawn furniture.

Baltimoreans are smarter than Denverites and she always ran into challenges when she tried "rip off tactics" here that she got away with in Denver, but she kept trying. My daughter was in the store with her, but came to the car complaining that she had a gut feeling her mother was about to do something stupid. I decided not to go into go into the store, but when she didn't come out for over an hour, I went in to check on her. Nicole spent half an hour asking why she couldn't keep her craziness in Denver, because one of her classmates might be working in the store.

When I went into the store, I couldn't find her, so I asked one of the clerks about her. The clerk called the store manager who advised me that she had been arrested for shoplifting. That night I went from the store to the police station to, to the county jail up trying to assure that she was released as soon as possible. I concocted a story about how her diabetes and the travel time after spending a twelve hour work day in Denver had left her in a mental stupor such that she was unaware of what she was doing. I did this to keep her out of jail, hoping all the while, that this was the situation that would stop her craziness. As usual she learned the wrong lesson and I realized that I had given her another wild card. She uses her health problems as a saber against less insightful persons who fall for her "poor me" drama.

The effect of not properly caring for her diabetes, starting to smoke again after over twenty years of not smoking and overindulging sweets, wine and beer, which is a way of life for her, has left her legally blind. She then used her visual handicap to worm $68,000 out of our insurance agent, who now realizes that he fell for her "poor blind person" drama!

Had he observed the furniture in the house, noticed that the locks on the doors required keys to get in, or out, listened, with care, to the conversation and realized that she, as usual was expensively dressed and able to put on her own make up; he might have saved his company some money.

When it is became imperative that I get a divorce, Jacquie became angry, saying that I was leaving her when she is down. For many years, I talked, I explained, I pleaded and she never listened, yet her response, like many female's was: "We don't communicate"! I asked , if she ever took advise from anyone who was involved in a stable relationship. Her sisters, friends and associates that I am aware of, should not give advice and she is the only one of her siblings who is in even a semi- stable relationship; and her friends are on a money, or image head trip. I went to counseling, and was selective about the professionals that I dealt with. I only accept advise from associates who are in viable relationships and putting effort into maintaining those relationships.

When I needed advice about my marriage, I went to Kaiser Permanente, and later an EAP Analyst that was provide by my company. I took my daughter so she could have private sessions. The one time I went to an analyst with Jacquie, that Jacquie chose, I got tired of the "You go girl", or "You are a Strong Black Women B.S" that filtered between conversations about big moneyed professional athletes and cute guys who made lots of money. It took months for the analyst and Jacquie to decide that Jacquie spent all the money that came into our household. I sometimes wonder, if they shared that tidbit of information with me, because they felt that they needed to tell me something to salve my "male ego". They came to this conclusion after I decided to go to other counseling with someone who was offering practical solutions. Jacquie always said that she did not need anyone telling her how to spend money, that she worked for, so I guess she went to an analyst that she could talk girl talk with.

I guess filing false insurance claims, and ripping off retail stores, her children, her dad and husband were part of her job description! She started telling me what friends, who never met me, or our children and female co workers, who had no men, and others, that she talk to, advise. She tells them what she wants them to hear and then revels in their girl talk responses, but those who have known us as a family tell very different stories. She never heard them, because she turned off her sensors when they advised her that she was destroying her family, her life and future.

A very enlightened young lady recently advised me that women usually blame breakups on other women, rather than face their failings as a mate, wife, or significant other. Jacquie's friends suggested that I, either had another woman, or I was gay! To all who wonder whether I ever had a mistress, the answer is no and that is a practical decision, because AIDS is on the rise among African American Females. It is not because the relationship with Jacquie was positive, since her only interest has always been in pleasing herself. Years ago I was told by male and female friends that I should have a lady on the side. When I thought about the other lady having someone on the side, I realized that side orders might get me a death sentence via a sexually transmitted disease. I am now trying to get my daughter through college and fortunately the small salary that I started with has grown, so I can now start to pay back student loans and help her to continue, if she decides to go for another degree. Times have been tough, but as I explained, I come from good stock and am up to handling challenges. I don't drink, smoke, or use illegal substances, and work hard, so I am healthy. Since the divorce my income has increased by over thirty percent, I have purchased a house, my credit is excellent and I took my brother and his wife to Cancun to stay in out timeshare at Royal Solaris Resort. Instead of shopping we did many things that I could never do, if Jacquie was along. Nicole now works and goes to school and I am planning a trip to Rio de Janeiro for November 2001.

Chapter 11

When I moved from full to part time, had no benefits, my car wasn't working and had to walk to work at night in mid winter, Jacquie got angry and suggested that I just didn't want to work I explained that I was changing my position, at the company, because under union rules I could top out in five years in my new position, while it would take ten, if I remained in my old job. Her father and brother suggested that I usually mapped out a process and probable knew what I was doing, but she became angry, suggested that I not use her company insurance. "She purchased a new Cadillac". She was already going to movies and dinner with male co workers and having house parties at home, but at no time did she consider me, or our daughter who was in college.

I overlooked her traits until I went to an analyst who gave me insights into my care taking habits. I became a facilitator for a woman who has serious character flaws and allowed her to halt my march toward my dreams and negatively impact my work, my business efforts and what I wanted for our children. I was always one to seek solutions and wanted a worthwhile relationship that was fulfilling for my family. I developed a Profile/Maintenance Test and a series of poems and got some of my associates to respond to it. I was pleasantly surprised when one of my coworkers suggested that he needed to take a look at himself, because he had some of the implied traits and a good woman that he might lose, if he didn't check himself. In many instances individuals saw problems with their mates, but never looked at themselves. Of course, my wife is in the latter group and suggested that I was lying and trying to put her down. My attempt was to send a serious message to those who were rearing children in dysfunctional families, because it is of no value to try and teach my children a set of rules, if parents have misplaced values.

I learned, early in my career, to develop solutions before discussing serious issues with business, social and political leaders. Caucasians who were in positions to effect change always asked: "What can I do to help", but I presumed that such a catch all question was a con and that they, either believed, or were hoping that I didn't have a clue, so I never visited with them until I had developed solution to problems, and a sales strategy for issues that I knew we were going to discuss. I was never been able to communicate cause/effect relationships to Jacquie, because solutions can only work when you care about consequences. If she is not getting what she wants, she just doesn't care! She goes to her sisters and scandalous girlfriends for encouragement, and disassociates herself from those who don't go along with her program. Anyone who happens to be heartless enough to tell her the truth is abruptly eliminated from her circle. She is in the game for herself and if you are faint at heart you will be taken advantage of. Those who are like her encourage her behavior until she, or they get used.

Our family's efforts were stymied by her low profile/high maintenance stature, so I fought on three fronts. I was challenged in my home, by the unethical job market that is omnipresent west of the Mississippi; and by my desire to grow and learn. As I became more aware of who I am, my opportunities diminished and my life at home became less tolerable.

Finally, I moved back to the east coast and found the support system that I left when I went from the military to California to Texas and Colorado. I, now, realize that true freedom is an intellectual process, and that my moral concepts will remain unaltered, if I refuse to buy into perceptions of success that harm my people, my community, my family, or myself! "I always wanted to own a business, because I wanted my children and my siblings' children to have options that I never had"! As long as I put all of my effort into surviving a corporate culture that has no respect for who I am and what I stand for, I will, forever, be struggling. If my significant other has no respect for my values, I am destined to lose. I always had a plan, but finally realized that my biggest challenge lived in my home, shared my bed, my income and children, and took all that we acquired for herself. I was spending too much time fighting the system and not recognizing I had been cut at the knees and started the gauntlet with a serious handicap

Jacquie filed false police reports, false insurance claims, bankruptcies and spent every dime the family earned. I made a final decision when I found that she had filed 11 claims against our auto insurance policy and $68,000 in claims against the homeowners policy and collected while my name was on the policy and checks. Later, Reggie's ex wife told me that she had once seen her come out of Reggie's Dad's bedroom in night clothes. It took her five years to tell me and she explained that she asked Reggie about the situation, when it happened, but he suggested that she just leave things alone. She says she later realized that Jacquie and I were still married and kept the information to herself until she felt that I should know. Jacquie isn't aware that I know and she, also, doesn't understand that I am angry about her asking her father to try to get me involved in defrauding the insurance company. The insurance agent explained that Reggie, was visiting from San Francisco, and moved items from different parts of the house to the dining room table, so he could view each individual piece that was to be insured on a floater policy. He explained that, exactly one year from that date she filed a claim.

She says that I treat her like a criminal, but overlooks my law enforcement past, my California Community College Instructors Certificate in Police Science and my attitude about lying and stealing. I told her father, that she never shared her acquisitions with me, or the children, so I was not going to get involved in scams that are against my principles. I discussed the possibility, with Reggie, that she was going to rip off the insurance company. After a conversation with the insurance agent I realized that he knew what was going to happen, long before I did.

I refused to lie and steal, to gain more material, for her. My destiny is to challenge life, so I will never cower, or cater to a woman who cares little about whether I, or my children, live the good life, or barely exist. Many of my former associates have gone to an early grave because unethical and distasteful acts gnawed at their insides, while their status implied healthy social lives. My next move was to make a decision about the marriage. I did not want a divorce, but she kept whittling away at my options. I remained in her house for many years to assure that my children were cared for and moved out just before Nicole completed high school, with plans to make a home for my daughter. She, long ago, excluded me from decisions about Reggie. I failed to teach him to drive fast, drink beer and smoke weed, so she taught him. She complained about his pot smoking, but had little concern about his alcohol intake! She smoked weed when he was a child and his uncle and dad smoke it, so why was she surprised? Children usually get bad habits from adults!

After I moved to Maryland, she had eight years to decide whether she wanted to be a wife and mother to me and our children versus one whose self interests ruled out any probability of our coming together as a viable family unit. She says that her girlfriend, whom I had not seen in twenty five years, said that I was evil and controlling and that she made me what I am today. On one occasion, after being admonished by one of her friend's husband, about her dating habits, she told me, while crying: "You should have controlled my crazy ass"!

When I met her I was a respected leader in San Francisco and being written about in periodicals from San Francisco to Minneapolis and Miami for developing quality and creative solutions that benefitted the community that I chose to serve. My associates were congressmen, the mayor and other business and social leaders from around the state. I was on the Boards of Directors of The Local development Company, The Southeast Law and Justice Taskforce, Southeast Education development and served as advisor to California's Coordinating Council for Higher Education and the Chancellor's Office for California's Community Colleges. In the years that I was with her I kept spiraling downward, but since moving back to Baltimore and away from her, I am once again finding respect for my ideas and ideals. When I go back to San Francisco I also get respect form those who knew me before her.

Her girlfriend, on the other hand has been successful with one of three children and the two who fell by the wayside were the males. The younger of the two boys has been in and out of jail since his early teens and the older is so demoralized that he no longer talks. Our first communication in over twenty years was a few years ago at her birthday party, where I met the male friend that Jacquie was going to San Francisco, "Using my travel privileges" to have lunch with. She never guessed that I knew him before I met her and remember when he worked at the post office on Third Street, while I was a patrolman in the Potrero District.

Her girlfriend's husband felt that it was okay to make me aware of each woman, present at the party, that he was sleeping with. When I suggested, to my sisters-in law, that it I was not interested in his bragging about his extra marital affairs, she queried: "Who Jacquie"! Somehow conversations with my in laws never come back as they are delivered, so I ended the discussion. They all have hearing problems.

Jacquie felt that it was okay to go to movies and dinner with male friends during our marriage and that such are not dates, because, as she explains, a date is when you sleep with someone. I agree, a date is when you sleep with someone, "If you are a prostitute"! For the rest of us, dinner and a movie is a date. If Jacquie wants dinner and movies with other men, she should have been anxious to get a divorce from me, because in such instances she is right: "I am controlling"! I want a woman who realizes that her actions reflect on our marriage and that it is not proper for a married partner to go to on dates with members of the opposite sex. I never asked for and will not tolerate an open marriage.

My in-laws are rearing males who are in and out of jail and females who are pregnant out of wedlock and in physical confrontations with aunts. The next generation has little respect for family elders, because they have not been shown good examples. The exception is my two children. She blames heredity for the way her nieces and nephews are, so the outcome is never the fault of her sisters. I watched them rear these children and predicted the outcome!

Chapter 12

Once Jacquie and I were married she responded negatively to almost every word I spoke, every thing I did, and all my needs and desires. She complains that I didn't call her sweet names, but never realized that her actions didn't justify sweet names. She is mean spirited, controlling, selfish and insensitive. I met her during a time when I was most confused. I was convinced that I had ruined Estelle's life, was going to school, putting too many hours into community work, and running a small college. I had a karate club, male and female basket ball leagues, a flag football team, film sessions in elementary schools, took youths on field trips, worked with the San Quentin Squires and the California Youth Authority: "Anything that I could do, I did"! I felt driven to do as much as I could and everybody was important. I had always thought that I was the black sheep of my family, so nothing I did was enough. I challenged the police department to do the right thing and I challenged others to work harder, but most of all, "I challenged myself".

I was insulted when one of my friends told me that I was a threat, because I was too honest and honest people snitch. He explained I was given the nickname Serpico by some fellow officers, but I had no idea who Serpico was: "I had a job to do and I was going to do it". I knew the difference between right and wrong and what I didn't know was guided by the law and statutes that I was taught to follow.

I was hurt when I heard one of the community workers say, in an open meeting, that I was a son of a bitch, but that I was honest. I asked: "Why he thought I was a son of a bitch", he explained that I expected others to work as hard as I worked and that he knew about my bouts with twenty four hour flu and how my body locked up because I was so driven and put in so many hours. I quickly realized: "No wonder I was driving Estelle crazy"! If others in the community saw me that way, why did she stay with me for five years.

My father had always said "I hate a liar and thief, and if you will lie, you will steal!" I knew that there was misuse of funds going on in community projects, lying in law enforcement and little accountability in most of the government programs, but I also knew that I was not a snitch, and I didn't want people to think of me as a son of a bitch. Was I was pushy and inconsiderate? I was surprised when it was implied that honest people tell on others. Hadn't I refused to pick up Shawn Bishop's Sister, when she shot and killed him after he hit her. I was surprised that I didn't get fired since the department knew that I could find her, if I really wanted to. Was I getting respect for doing the right things, or anger from those that I was trying to help?

I was bothered that some policemen were more concerned with making arrests than finding out who had really committed crimes and many teachers were more concerned about paychecks than teaching. My effort was to keep myself clean, accountable, practical and working for: " The betterment of my people and my community". I was driven to do for too many people and should have worked harder at doing things for and with Estelle.

Chapter 13

I was going to school and accumulating credits, because I knew, at a gut level, that I would lose some of my community status, if I put in for a degree. The California Mentality is to keep you down rather than encourage you to go forward, so I was elated when Jacquie suggested that it was time to move on and go for the degree. I got my Degree in August and by September I started hearing negative statements from the people that I had worked hard to help. "You used to be good people, then you went and got that darned degree; now you use all those big words and you've gotten to be to good for yourself!" "You were a good policeman, but you have changed!"

All my efforts were challenged, so I had no choice, but to move on!

I now knew why they all gave by friend Charlie such a hard time. I often called him a walking encyclopedia and respected his education, but community residents that liked me, treated him with disrespect. "I needed to move on to bigger and better things" and it was Jacquie who convinced me to take the LSAT and GRE and go to law, or graduate school. She got took some of the courses that I developed for the community and worked with me on some of the projects that I was involved in, but once we were married everything changed and the supportive Jacquie disappeared!

Later, she was quick to say, "I don't want to talk about that, or we have already discussed that, and tries to control everything that is discussed. She critiqued me and the children on what to say and when to say it, while her conversation got very tacky. The one conversation that I hate is about a time when she asked one of her bosses, "Who do I have to f—to get a raise in this company"! Another is about when she arrived at work and someone asked about her hair to which she replied: "What, do I look like someone f—ed my brains out"! Miss "I know I have class" makes this kind of statement in mixed company, but wants to tell us how and when to talk.

During one of my last visits to Colorado, we had a conversation with one of her co workers and his friend. The two came to a get together and spent the afternoon trying to find out what kind of a man I am. I knew that I was being observed, but when she explained the, Who do I have to f—to get a job scenario, I felt the energy of their scrutiny. From that point on both men frequently injected: "How does Bill feel about that" when she made asinine statements?

I mentioned, during the discussion, that I had always dreamed of owning a U shaped ranch style house that sat on a hill surrounded by a white fence and that I wanted four horses, because I wanted two children. Jacquie's response was "I never knew that you had such a dream and you have never been on a horse"! I responded: "Now isn't that interesting, after all these years you never knew"! The two guys responded: "That is interesting" and gestured to each other! My daughter entered the room and said: "I always knew that was Dad's Dream", once again the two men gestured each at the other! One stated, "Enough said", to which the other responded, "Right on"!

Jacquie has always done for Jacquie, so the children and I were destined to lose. She has recently stated, she was happy doing as she has done, so I suggested that she used all the family's resources on herself. Her response was "I am a doer"! "There is no justification for getting married, bringing children into the world and taking advantage of their existence!

One night I went to a club in Port Arthur, Texas with Jacquie, a young lady that I had never met before and one of her friends that my daughter and I call "Art a Fake", because she gambled her way out of a marriage. Jacquie raves about the fact Artie Fay now has a man who gives her money, so she can gamble whenever she wants to. When she and Artie Fay left the table the young lady explained that Jacquie and I seemed different as night and day. she surmised that I appeared very conservative, but that Jacquie was all about money and like Artie Fay, could care less about a man's feelings! I had heard similar comments from other women, but this was a young lady who knew that she would probably never see me again. I was impressed, because of what I knew about Artie Fay. I had become accustomed to male bashing, whining, scheming women when I went on trips to Texas with Jacquie, and one of the worst was an aunt. Comments in her yearbook should have been a sign, but I surmised that most had probably grown since high school: "They had not".

Most who know me will suggest that I am not religious man, but a very spiritual man. Put simply, I believe that God is either in your total being, or not in you at all, and you can not resolve the issue of your relationship with a higher power by talking the talk and going to church one day a week to make up for the dirt you do the other six days. I also refuse to believe that you can knowingly do dirt most of your life and be saved. Too many people believe that we can be saved a multitude of times, because god loves us unconditionally. The implication is that God is stupid.

I try to live by and teach my children based on the ten commandments because I feel that they are an excellent set of standards. My children have not spent years among organized religionist, but I have taught them to do the right thing by setting a good example. Both are good, descent human beings and I feel that I have fostered their spiritual growth. There have been times, when I have lowered my guard, and gone along with their mother's crazy activities, but when I realized what I was doing wrong, I regrouped and told myself I was better than that. I tried to help nieces and nephews in any way that I could, because in her family there is no cooperative effort.

Her brother lived with us in Dallas, her sister lived with us in San Leandro and her brother lived with us again in Oakland. Her brother would watch the kids during times when neither of us was at home, because he and I had difficulty finding work. Jacquie complained that there were White Males and Black Females on the bus, when she went to work and wondered why most of the Black Males didn't have jobs. Her sisters were so hard on the brother that I suggested that he go to Los Angeles and stay with my brother and sister in law. I later found out that he tried to hit on my sister in law while he was living with them. I now understand why he talks so ugly about my sister in law who has become one of my favorite friends and family members. It is a family trait that they try to shame those who see through their veil of B.S.!

Chapter 14

When I first met Jacquie, I was president of an education project, that I had developed. I always felt that I had to develop my own strategy and that a private enterprise was probably the only real option that would allow me to fulfill my dreams. I wanted more than a low paying job that I could be fired from on a whim. I wanted to use my GI Bill to invest in apartment buildings that I could collateralize into additional units. More than anything, I wanted her to understand, so there would be no conflict. The understanding never came, money kept flowing through her hands and I kept getting losing opportunities.

Jacquie wanted it all, for herself, and was willing to sacrifice me and the children. She was ill mannered, selfish and aggressive, but not competent, or skilled. Companies were comfortable with her go along to get along attitude because it is perceived that such selections don't effect the bottom line, and they know that is easy to fire less capable minorities. When they finally decided to terminate her I used their past practices against them, but in the end she benefitted and, once again, the children and I lost. She got a settlement, a big raise and an attitude that was worse than before.

At the last class reunion that I attended with her she seemed intent upon letting her classmates know that she was making more money and had a bigger house than they, but her arrogance didn't stop there. She felt that she had outgrown all of our other family members, so her already bad attitude got worse. To quote her: "I am not looking back", so she became too good to visit my brother's apartment, because he didn't have what she had. Of course the infighting within her family got worse and she steered clear of my family. She had the good judgment to know that while her family bickers, my family "kicks ass", so she steered the right course. Nieces and nephews, on her side of the family, like many Black Youth, need to face the fact that the reason for their anger resides in their own homes. Parents sold out for "Temporary Access" to fine clothes, big cars, and nice houses.

Better educated children are more visionary and feel that they have a right to work for "Access and Control" of a piece of the national pie. Many parents fail to teach children what is going on in the real world, because they are "themselves" in denial. Generation X is seeing down sizing, hostile takeovers, a general lack of opportunity and realizing that they need a set of rules that work for them. I tried to get my children to understand that there are other options and my daughter is moving in a direction that I feel with benefit her. Like her cousins from my side of the family, she in college and planning her future.

I was a planner and always looked to the future, so my daughter is doing as I have done. My ex wife can only see what she can touch, so I was her conscience, her baby sitter, her caretaker and "unfortunately" a facilitator, thus, she surmised that I would be there, regardless of her actions. She thwarted my efforts while raving about how fine Magic Johnson, L.T., Spike Lee, or some other "perceived to be rich" male was and was quick to advise me what friends who made more money than I were thinking She never understood that we can never have money, if she spends it all on herself, or that once money is spent "it is gone"! The friends that she quoted, usually suggested, to me, that "She" is my problem.

She lives in a realm that is not of this earth. One day she came home and told me that one of her Male coworkers had questioned her about a picture of Denzel Washington that she had framed and displayed on her desk. I tried to explain that "maybe" her coworker, like most people, feel that it is inappropriate to have another man's photo on your desk when you are married. She immediately became argumentative and, later, changed the story to: "I became angry when I came to the office and saw Denzel's Photo on her desk. "I have never seen the photo", but knew that whomever she chose to leave me for would have relieved me of a massive, excedrine headache.

When I started developing the manuscript for this book I sent it out to my sister in law, and asked her to tell me whether she noticed any of the habits that I was writing about. She called me the very next day and told me that she had waited eighteen years to tell me what she thought, and that I may be sorry that I asked. She explained that she always felt that her family lost, because of my marriage to Jacquie, because she knew that I was as committed to extended family as I was to my immediate family. She stated that she was jealous that I gave my wife so much attention and that I should develop a course to teach men how to love a women. She went on to explain that Jacquie did not appreciate being with a sensitive, caring man and that she often thought about introducing me to other women. Later close family friends offered similar comments.

As I wrote I decided to send Jacquie some of the writings. She told me that I was writing a bunch of lies, that my sister in law was nothing but a whore and she never wanted to see her again. What will she say when she finds out what Luisa, Tony and Bruni, our former tax accountant, insurance man, Loretta and other friends have to say. She has told me what people that don't know me say, once she tells them her side of the story, but I have only listened to those who have known us and the children as a family for many years. I never asked for the information, they decided to tell me.

I started listened when Tony suggested that I needed to begin to protect my finances, and that I needed to see Jacquie as she really is. I was surprised by their comments, but realized that close friends saw more than I was willing to admit. She complains that they all stopped coming around when she lost her eyesight, but the truth is that they stopped coming around as soon as the children and I left the house.

She is smart enough to pick nice folks and make up untruths for female associates. She chooses women who are angry and willing to accept that all men are bad, but If someone challenges her information, she avoids further contact. Female associates who listen to mythological nonsense usually conclude that I am guilty, because: "That's how men are"!

She told me that the lady who sells Shaklee Products, said that the first time we met, I gave her this evil stare. I guess she felt that the best way to sell her product was to say something bad about me. Jacquie seldom says good things, about me, so the Shaklee Lady probably sensed that she could to get more business by going along with the program.

Chapter 15

She never realized that getting a divorce was my only alternative. I explained that her habits were destroying my opportunities to buy property in Baltimore, start a small business, or finance a car for our daughter to attend college. In 1993 the City of Baltimore was prepared to make me loan me $70,000 and the manager of a business incubator offered an additional $20,000, if I would develop my enterprise at his site, until they found the bankruptcy, that she filed in 1987. In 1997 our daughter and I went to Denver to try to buy a car and were told, in her presence, that she was 150 days behind on her VISA Account, and almost as far behind on a Sears Account, so financing was refused. At that time she explained that she had been angered, because a credit union would not finance her new Cadillac, so she stopped making payments on the VISA Account. During the divorce I found that she was only behind on accounts where my name was included.

She explained that she was upset when I wouldn't take over a $517 per month car note on the Cadillac when she could no longer drive it because it was determined that she is legally blind. Her salary was 2.5 times mine, when she purchased it and she felt that it was important to buy luxury items, while I felt that it was important to pay our daughter's college expenses.

I never thought that I would be so angry with the woman that I felt was perfect twenty six years ago, but after begging for answers, listening to inane talk shows, reading books that are sold to make money rather than deal with serious issues, going to a female analyst that spent half of the session talking about Alex English, L.T., Magic Johnson, and Denzel Washington; I got fed up and found an analyst that was ready to make real suggestions about our marriage. She stayed with the original lady and has said that she went to her to resolve problems that she was having at work. I suggested that we were at the same dance and her problems at home were more serious than her problems at her job. The reality was that she has having a problem with life because she lives in a fantasy world! Today, I am convinced that she is not confused and that she is living up to her satanic purpose! "She is here to destroy and self destruct"!

The group session that I sat in included policemen, pilots, firemen and many professions, but I was the only Black. All of the participants had more problems than I and all had better paying jobs and more secure futures. I quickly realized that I was stronger, more aware and better off than the entire group, so I cut my visits short, because I did not want to use company funds to play mind games and buy books that I had already read while studying psychology as an undergraduate at San Francisco State.

She made small gestures at trying to share, but selfishness and impulse usually took charge again and she continued what is a way of life for her. Her nature is to take from whomever she get an opportunity to take from. If she stays in a hotel, she will leave with towels, dishes, silverware, coffee pots, or whatever she feels that she wants. She has serious control issues and does not believe in constructive criticism, because she has no interest in reality, or morality.

All I ever wanted was to be a good husband, father, lover and friend in times when responsibility is out, love is out, caring is out, and materialism is in. I ultimately went back to my roots, and talked to my sisters, my aunts, and cousins. The women that I grew up with and learned from as a child saved me and made me whole again. I grew up thinking that all women were precious and ultimately fell prey to a crazy, selfish female. I wanted to believe that humans are basically good, but I now feel that we need rules just to make humans treat one another like people. I wanted to feel that women were precious again, so I visited my Aunt Perneller and my Aunt Sis, the elder states women in my family. Like my grandmother and the rest of my aunts these women have dignity and humility. Jacquie believes habits that get her nieces and nephews into trouble are inherited from the fathers, so it is not her sister's fault that her boys have been to jail for drugs, pimping and credit card fraud. When her nieces battered her sister, she refused to accept the idea that they might be getting even for things that her sister did to them. It is the fault of the father that they have not known since they were very small, so to quote her: "They are just like their father"!

I found that one of my best resources was my youngest sister who was hesitant to get involved in something as serious as my marriage, but explained that she never visited our home in Colorado, because Jacquie kicked our brother out when he was out of a job and had no place to go. She felt that she should have talked to him when I was present, and not waited until I was gone to tell him that he had to go. I explained that I came close to filing for a divorce at that time, but realized that I couldn't leave the children. I was packing my books, when my seven year old, daughter asked me not to go. My wife's brother and sister lived with us and I never asked them to leave. When her brother left, after his second stay with us, he moved in with one of my brothers and his wife.

Jacquie is a natural decorator, so our well heeled friends comment about how well she handles design. One of our associates joked about the fact that we had the only color coordinated house among the Jack and Jill

Families, and when we had parties most of her friends would show up to see what new idea she had developed. Some of the less talented women tried to copy her ideas in their homes and showed twinges of jealousy, because they wanted to be the center of attention. One friend was so catty that she not only tried to out do Jacquie in her own home, but would take her animosity to work and tell lies about me to cause problems between us. Jacquie would come home and start arguing, as was her way, never accepting the possibility that I never talked to her crazy friends. Her talents and patience were not wasted on me, or the children.

There were times when she knew that she had gone overboard and would send cards, or buy clothes, for me, that she liked. Of course she would try to dictate when, where and how I should wear the clothes. Her other approach was to cry and say that I was being mean to her. One of her favorite games was to suggest that I should weigh advantages against the disadvantages of staying with her. Her only advantage was that she was the mother of my children!

She is going through life's changes having medical problems, and has suggested that I am leaving when she is down, but my decision to move on is based on many years of insanity and my patience is gone. We lived apart for almost a decade, which I feel is ample time to fix marital problems, if one is serious about doing the right thing. Her medical condition has now become a weapon that she uses against unsuspecting victims, like our insurance agent, but my primary concern is about the impact on our children. I feel obligated to provide them with an explanation about their relationship with us and I believe that it is imperative that I guide them into the future with good information. There are solutions once we understand the problems.

She is relatively successful in the White World and has openly stated that she will never again live in a predominantly Black Environment. We prefer different worlds and the rules change once choices are made. As in many Black Families she, gets the opportunity and I get the blues. I have the education and skills, am underpaid and overworked, but I am from good, strong stock and will overcome. The blues ain't nothin, but a color.

Chapter 16

Our first two years were like a dream, so I felt as if I would always be with her. But, we married May 18, 1973 and by June 1973 the dream turned to a nightmare. It was as if I was now living with a total stranger and I didn't have a clue as to whom she was. I decided that she was different, because she was pregnant, but the changes remained until I filed for the divorce. The situation improved for brief periods, when she was feeling poorly, but when she was healthy she exhibited negative, almost pathological, behaviors. She has different memories, and says that she was not unhappy, but her memory conveniently comes and goes, so she never has to face her demons. She showed that she was unhappy by criticizing my integrity, my ideas, my honesty, my business plans, the way I talked, what I talked about, who I talked to and everything that I did. The beginning of the end started the day we were married

Our sex life soured by of 1973, and in later years she often, physically, kick me out of bed if I touched her and she didn't want to be touched. When she was ready for sex I was supposed to be ready to respond and she concluded that when she was satisfied, I was satisfied. She would say things like "That was wonderful" and go to sleep! She says that our sex life was great, told me that she had her first orgasm with me, and that she had told her girlfriends how good it was. Still, she often told me that I couldn't kiss her, because I would then want to have sex. Later, she said that I will make love to her, but will not kiss her.

One example of just how crazed this relationship is occurred during a weekend that she planned for us in Breckenridge. We ended up in a suite with a whirlpool tub in the master bedroom and I planned to take full advantage of what was to be a very romantic situation. I purchased a full body suit that exposed her curves but had openings in all the right places. After a stint in the hot tub, I moisturized and massaged her body, helped her into the body suit and went about showing her why it was designed that way. She murmured that she missed all this good treatment and that I should be there to do it more often. Once she reached orgasm I moved close to her to caress her. I had not yet entered her, because I wanted to make this a night of pleasure. She abruptly left the bedroom and went into the living room where our daughter was watching tv. Later she came back to bed, piled pillows and blankets between us and went to sleep. Each time I attempted to touch her she pushed me away. The following night she piled blankets and pillows between us, but had wanted her feet massaged during that day. I decided that I was not going to spend my vacation as I had spent the past twenty years. Once we got back to Denver I took an early flight to Baltimore.

She never seems to understand that our interaction hinges on the past. She wants to forget her actions, and tells me that she will never again be with a man that doesn't want things, while she never had a clue about anyone's want or needs, but her own. Her craziness impacted our sex life, but she failed to understand why I was upset when she purchased sex toys claiming that I was not there to satisfy her needs. I explained that she didn't have enough appetite for me under normal circumstances, so why did she need tools that will make my efforts more difficult. She then said that the tools were too hard and unnatural: "After being with a man for so many years". She failed to understand that electronic stimulators are like drugs. You eventually need to increase the dosage to get little satisfaction. On one occasion, she took the sales persons advise and pressed a small vibrator against my penis while I was inside her. This caused me to lose my normal control and ejaculate too quickly, ruining what could have been a pleasant evening. She purchased a book about how to keep your women begging for more, and since I saw it on the stairs, I read it and asked her about it. She explained that it was a waste of money and that we really didn't need the book. I sat there wondering: "What in the world is goes on inside her head"!

There were times, in early years, when I judged our sexual frequency by her monthly period. If we had not had sex by that time of the month, I knew I would have to wait at least another week. Many was the time when we went five and six weeks with no sex. Eight to ten times a year is not my idea of a great sex life, so I learned to just run a bath tub full of hot water, masturbate and fall asleep in the tub. By the time I woke up I was usually so tired that it didn't matter. This went on for years, so I realized that the person that I married was not the warm loving woman that I enjoyed for two years!

The disrespect also started in late 1973. One day we had invited her best friend and some of her associates to our apartment for a little get together. One of the guys lied all evening about his financial accumulations, as is typical of some California men. He owned seven eleven's and had fancy cars, but the underlying truth was that he drove a bus. My wife asked, "Why don't you find me a man with some money!" Her sister and friends claim not to have heard her statement, and she now claims that she did not make it, but at the time, I asked her to step out of the room and she defended it saying that she was grown.

The one thing that I always hated about California Women was their love of money and their lack of respect for real values, and here was the women that I had married, being shallow and gullible. Why had she been so different during the first two years. It wasn't enough that I knew that the guy was lying, but my wife who challenged everything that I tried to do was buying into the most common con in California.

When I first got to California my buddies, who were mostly from the east, would tell jokes about naive, money hungry California Women. Many would brag about how often they were scoring, by talking about money, renting big cars, or lying about their jobs. I worked for a company that sold bibles and encyclopedias when I was dating Angie. My White boss would bring two Black woman from Los Angeles to San Francisco, each weekend, and brag that he could sleep with any Black Woman by offering her money. He then suggested that he could even sleep with Angie, if he offered the right price. When his Scandinavian cousins visited San Francisco and one of suggested that she wanted to go out with me he had a fit. I bragged that "I didn't offer her any money.

During those years I played semipro basketball and one of my teammates bet me that he could get this girl to sleep with him if he gave her the two dollars that she needed to get into a Jackie Wilson Concert. He had her in the back seat of a car with all of us watching, so to hear my wife, who wasn't satisfying my needs, fall for that con was really disheartening. I later realized that she wasn't falling for a con: "She is as scandalous as the women that we complained about and would later complain that: "Black Men just aren't devious enough"!

I had a tough time finding work, after returning from grad school, in Texas, as did most who were committed to civil rights in the sixties. I got as little respect from home as I did from an unfair racist system. I was educated, competitive, committed and had integrity that matched my skills, so the system made me pay for not bowing and accepting unethical practices that were prevalent in California. Whites who were committed to a better America, gave money, product services, and themselves, while others decided that we were troublemakers and worked against us. We were treated as poorly by Blacks who benefitted from discrimination as we were by Whites who fought against change.

Chapter 17

In my lifetime, I have known and associated with big guns, including congressmen, senators, mayors and business executives, but because of my ideals about the laws of the universe and right versus wrong, I lived much of my life on the fringe of poverty. The question that I ask myself is: "Has my stay on this rock been a benefit, or a deficit to mankind? I am happy with who I am and what I have done with my life, even though I could have done more. One wrong decision impacted twenty years of my life, but the fact that I am healthy and strong, means that I have an opportunity to make corrections. I have considered going back to school to study dyslexia and autism, so I can work with children in the primary grades. I think that I might better serve my country by assisting those who have not become immersed in the totality of our sickness.

After graduation from San Francisco State I thought that I might become an attorney and continue my struggle against civil rights violations. Thurgood Marshal made the statement that the one place where we could challenge an unjust system was via the law, in the courts. We moved to Dallas in 1973 with the idea that I would go to law school, become a police officer and work my way through. I have a California Community College Instructors Certificate, an Advanced, Peace Officers Standards and Training Certificate, four years of military police training, two years as a campus policeman, five years with the S.F.P.D. and background investigations for the military, the S.F.P.D. and the U.S. Justice Department. A reduction in force eliminated the job opportunity with the Justice department, but the background check became an advantage, when I was denied a job with the Dallas Police Department.

I enrolled in graduate school applied, but found that I was unemployable in Dallas, because the city was years behind on issues of civil rights. The D. A. gave a lecture on how to keep minorities and females off juries, and I complained that his statements were unconstitutional, but was rebuffed by a Black Male Student who advised me that I was forgetting where I was. It was in Dallas that I realized that it takes more than money to make a good parent and that it is necessary for power mongers and controllers to have a cadre of, go along to get along fools, for a system to function to the detriment of citizens who pay taxes for benefits that they will not receive. A system also needs fools who happen to be Black, Hispanic and female to function against Black, Hispanics and females.

Jacquie asked a Jewish Friend from the Justice department to check and see why I was not hired by the Dallas Police Department, because she was concerned about the attitude of the investigator who came to our home. The Justice Department Official, knew Chief Dyson and was able to get my file and prove that the investigator put false information in my record. It turned out that he did not like my civil rights involvement in California and could not fathom my becoming a member of his department. Even worse, many of the African Americans that I frequently communicated with, had inside information, but were afraid to tell me what they knew.

I had taken law courses en route to my Associates Degree in criminology and felt that my studies had set the tone about how to fight discrimination and the abuse of power, until a Dallas Friend explained that I really got my philosophy from my upbringing along the eastern seaboard. He surmised that Blacks who were born in the east had a different attitude about freedom than those who lived west of the Mississippi. He spent eight years in Southern California, got his first degree from U.S.C., traveled extensively and noticed the differences during his travels. I have become convinced, as he that Blacks from the east are more cohesive and stronger on issues of civil rights, family, politics and economics.

My friend and the Justice Department Official who interviewed me, suggested that I needed to leave Dallas, or learn to accept the fact that Texans weren't ready for my way of thinking. Californians, Coloradans and my ex wife were unprepared for my "PROUD OF BEING BLACK" philosophy! My training in social learning theory taught me that the job market would be tough as long as I maintain high standards and respect my ethnicity, but my courses in behavior modification gave me alternatives, so I started learning how to live with a different approach to life. Near the end of our marriage, Jacquie suggested that running a business has always been the answer for me, but never accepted the reality that spending all of our available capital, filing bankruptcies and insurance fraud hindered my progress.

Chapter 18

In September 1973 we moved back to California and I took a job with a company that tested my ethics, but taught me about sales and management, family values and how companies can play an unethical spouse against a good employee. I won the first five sales contest, but my commissions were never correct. I was quickly promoted to the interview team and on to Regional Director, but found that the company was more concerned about my law enforcement past. At one point I got a call from the California Department of Real Estate asking that I assist with an investigation of the company. I refused, because I got enough flack about my civil rights past while in Dallas and did not need to, now, be recognized as a snitch. Much of our nation's corporate structure is insensitive to strong, talented minority professionals, so I was not going to dig myself deeper into a pit of underemployment. I respect Omnivest as the smartest company that I ever worked for, but they were a bunch of crooks who went into and out of business every three years. They perfected their strategy to a level that I had never seen before, or since. I often wonder why "Legitimate" companies aren't as smart.

The company lawyer helped me, because I had brought he and a Black Female that he was in love with, but did not know how to contact, together. Apparently someone in the office heard me mention the lady's name and told him that I knew her. He was concerned about asking for my help, but one of my coworker suggested that I was open minded and that he should just ask. When he approached me I told him that I would have to insure that she didn't mind, and when I talked to her she asked me not to tell him that she would be coming to his next lecture.

When she walked into the class it was obvious that they belonged together: "He couldn't wait to finish his class and she was as anxious as he". As I walked out of the class he stopped me, offered thanks and asked me to meet with him the next day. That next day he gave me a history lesson on the company and it's management concepts. He explained that they couldn't afford to irritate me, because I was their best "minority" example of success, but was not to be trusted, because I had integrity, a law enforcement past, was able to communicate with clients that many of the best sales people had a hard time with; and I had respect from city leaders.

On one occasion I had Jayatirtha Das and Bakta Das from the Krishna Religious Movement come in as potential investors. In developing a profile, I found that they ran an incense factory in Southern California that brought in eleven million in profits the year prior and that Bakta Das, alone, had sold $139,000 in trinkets that same year. I set an appointment and felt that I had enough rapport to sell each a parcel of land, but someone else read the profile and set an earlier meeting time. I walked into the office as the Krishna's were walking out and could feel the tension. Bakta and Jayatirtha Das stopped for a brief moment, shook my hand and advised: "Bill you are a good man, but you need to take a serious look at the people you work for"!

I, now, realized that the company was monitoring everything that I did. I outsold their best sales people and proved my interview and management skills. This company watched my every move, but had not had a Black Salesman do as well as I, so I became a lesson in how to get into the pockets of Blacks! They had no reason to fire me, were smart enough to know that I was bringing in a lot of money and that bad publicity would ruin their process, so they watched and learned. I also watched and learned!

I called each of my clients and advised them to not sell the land regardless of media reports, since I now knew how the scheme worked and how to assure that my clients benefitted. We were doing three million dollars per month in the San Francisco Office and the Southern California Offices made even more money. The company sold raw land for three years, filed bankruptcy and let the media do the rest. The land was held in a subsidiary of a major bank, recouped and sold again and again until it was ready to be developed. I purchased a piece of land, but Omnivest kept the deed, so I lost it when I left the job. The company made payments on my car and the land, as long as I was on payroll, but I lost access to the deed, during the bankruptcy. I was owed $60,000 in commissions, but knew that I would never collect, because the company knew, and I knew, that my greatest adversary was my wife. One of the managers offered me an opportunity to move with him to a Walnut Creek Office, to set up a similar activity, but I had learned my lesson. For those of you who have seen the film: "The Boiler Room", Omnivest was a boiler room, and I was Damn Good, but not stupid enough to continue.

Now Bruce, the other Black Manager was an interesting character. He had been a school teacher, but liked working in one of San Francisco's finest high rise office complexes and driving the new Cadillac that was provided as long as he went along with the plan. As a Director he, like myself, was to receive commissions from consultants that he managed. He did as he was told and prior to my coming to the company was the only prominent Black employee. When we visited him at his apartment and his wife, Gladys, would start fussing, he would find a newspaper, and go sit in the bathroom. My wife thought that was the cutest story and told it to all of her lady friends.

One night he invited us to a Richard Pryor Concert. Every time he asked me a question about work that I knew that I shouldn't answer, I would respond, such that I could avoid the question, but Jacquie would responded: "That's not what he asked you"! It was as if there were three friends in the car and I was the outsider. I never got the same considera-tion at work after that night and guessed that the company knew that I would have to go it alone, if I was to litigate against them. They started stealing my client list and I became accustomed to coming into the office and meeting my clients on the way out. The company developed a strat-egy to eliminate my effort to challenge them.

Jacquie also perfected her strategy. She played naive and not too bright, cried at the right time and uses her womanhood like a sword to whittle away anything that stands in the way. Beneath her exterior is a game plan that can be as damaging as an arctic winter. She has now garnered an even more deadly weapon: "Her declining health". Omnivest management found, through conversation with Bruce, that she would do anything for a dollar, and as the lawyer friend stated: "This company will control you by taking advantage of your spouse' lack of integrity "!

I left Omnivest knowing, that I was as much a pigeon as were my investors. I knew that they would resurface again, but I also realized how smart they were, so I wasn't going to waste time trying to litigate against them. The lawyer explained what I needed to do to recoup my losses, but suggested that the company knew that I wouldn't have the support of my wife. Omnivest gave me something that money can't buy: "I left knowing that I can compete with the best and brightest, and how far some, includ-ing Jacquie, will go to get money".

My next position was with Evelyn wood Reading Dynamics and I was out of town for two to four weeks at a time, which didn't bother me a lot, because my home life was stifling and I was finding, from other women, when I traveled, that I wasn't so bad. The upside was that whenever I got back into town Jacquie was romantic and sexual, rather than cold and aloof as she was when I was in town all the time. She signed me up to take a test for The San Jose Police Department to keep me closer to home, but the medical examiner claimed that I had a back ailment, and conveniently lost my back x-rays. The department had been charged with discrimination and had to fill each academy class with fifty percent minorities. They met the hiring quota, but most never completed probation. I paid a "Black Lawyer" six months advance payments, based on a agreement for $200 per month, but he sent me a statement requesting more money, or he couldn't take my case. He then skipped town! I chose him, because I believe in supporting minority professionals: "I chose wrong"!

Jacquie, on the other hand, did the right thing, because women were coming out of the woodwork. I had a tough time getting women to leave my hotel room after we completed the paperwork. In Memphis, one student from "Ole Miss" would come to all of my lectures, sit in the front row and stare, while others would remain in my suite, where I completed my paperwork, until everybody else left and make their moves. In Buffalo, New York a student told her boyfriend that she was going to come to my hotel room and see, if I was as good as she thought I could be, and a White

College Student refused to give me her $395 tuition unless I kissed her. Jacquie called while she was there, so I started talking on the phone, but she just sat and waited. I started to think that I should have a lover on the side, if I was going to stay with Jacquie, but decided that I had made enough of a mess of Estelle's Life and would move on rather than start sleeping around.

The trend of women approaching me worsened when they met Jacquie. Women seem to know that she only cares about herself, so I had offers and dares from women who suggested that they would treat me better. I made the decision that I was not going anywhere until my children were grown!

Jacquie showed commitment to material and shocked me on an occasion when her sister took a $25,000 check from the bank that she worked for. She and an older sister planned to cash in on these ill gotten gains, so they became unusually helpful. Jacquie cooked a big pot of spaghetti, which was an expensive ordeal, because she always put a lot of special meats and seasonings into spaghetti. It turned out that the sister wouldn't even pay for the spaghetti, so they hurled profanity at each other; she from the street and her sister from the third level of her apartment building. I couldn't believe what I was seeing and hearing. I tried to explain that a felony had been committed and that the FBI was going to come after her sister. Not the San Francisco Police: "The FBI"!

The next sign of a problem was when I walked in on her buying furs that she knew we couldn't afford. Years later when we discussed the furs and she explained that she paid for them with her money. The truth is that they were part of her planned, first bankruptcy filing. My argument was that people usually get together when they are going to make major expenditures, if they intend to be together. I argued that she always spent what ever amount on what ever item she wanted and we can't survive under such rules. Throughout our marriage, when I mentioned her spending habits, she always responded, "I work too"! In later years it became "I spend my money." We were never a team and any response from me was just coincidental. Still, she wonders why I left.

One day, after I had moved to Baltimore, I visited with her in Denver and she was trying on a pair of pants. She complained that she didn't like The pants. I responded "They look good on you," to which she replied "I didn't ask for your opinion!" When I advised her about that ugly response she stated " I spent my money on these pants." I quickly realized that was why I left and I sure as hell wasn't coming back to that kind of ugliness. Days later, when she called and said that she was willing to go to a marriage counselor to make the marriage work, I ignored the concept, because I know in my heart that I have given all that I have to give over too many years.

She never had to fight the good fight, because things came too easy. She never questioned the motives of her demons, because she got what she wanted. She had material, supportive sisters and girlfriends, but the most important thing in her life was her house in which she sheltered her materials. She broke all of the rules, destroyed her health and her relationship with me and the children. I stopped listening to what she said and started watching what she did, and once our children were grown I moved away from her. She should never have considered marriage, because she is not a team player and marriage is about teamwork. To this day I hear men talk about former girlfriends who are like her and they explain that: "Women like her use men until they are broken, or in jail, and after each they move on to the next, forgetting about the last"! I wonder why she stayed? I damn sure wasn't going to let her break me!

Now, she is legally blind and has more money than we ever had, when she could drive, shop and spend, spend, spend. When she became upset and explained that I was not supportive, I suggested that I will be supportive when her conclusions make sense to me. I was truthful when I told her that she was doing things that damaged our family, but I didn't advise her, because I learned that she must do her own thing. I answered questions when she asks for my opinion, but realized that marriage was a convenience, because of insurance and travel benefits that she got from my job. I had no greater expectations.

She was quick to remind me that she talked to her sister, because she was supportive and I respond that her sister is like her and makes feel good decisions that hurt in the long run. Her sister moved to Atlanta to find a "southern man", but fails to understand that her habits will cause conflict with any man of substance, just as they did when she lived in California. A change of venue is only good, if one is willing to eliminate unnecessary baggage. Unless there are drastic changes, she will be alone, in Georgia, as they are all alone, in Texas, or California. They are alone, even when they are in relationships, because they are selfish, overbearing, unrealistic and scandalous.

We are, both diabetic, but the fact that I make adjustments has helped me to become successful in fighting this challenge. She has gone from type two to insulin dependent, while I exercise and changed my diet to assure that I remain type two. She fails to understand that her tendency toward excess is, her real enemy, as are female associates who listen to her stories and say "You go girl" without benefit of facts. There are the men who want to bed her and are willing say anything, or use any means to discredit me, and there are men who wonder why I don't live with her, because she is a good looking woman. She loves material, images and excess and refuses to understand that her love affair with things has destroyed all that she could have been! To quote my sister "She seems like a nice person, but she is confused, and some people take their confusion to the grave"! She gets advice from some very caring people, some who don't care, and siblings who are as unethical as she. I continue to do seek positive alternatives to help build a bridge to the future for me and the children.

Chapter 19

In 1997 I made a trip to Denver to get her to go to a marriage counselor as she promised. I had been trying to get her to go for years and she finally agreed. I had three hours to do some visiting, so I dropped by our old tax accountant's office. I had not seen Ron and Kathy for many years and they had not done our taxes, since she told Jacquie that her spending habits were destroying the family finances. The first question from Kathy was "how is Jacquie"? I explain that I had been in Maryland for six and a half years and I was in town to either fix our marriage or seek closure. When Ron walks into the room she restated my response to which he replied "bluntly"! "I am surprised that it lasted this long"!

I left his office and drove to Northglenn to visit another friend that I had not talked to in a while. Tony is Puerto Rican and has been on military disability for many years, so we start off talking about his fiftieth birthday and the fact that he contracted asthma when he stopped smoking. We were talking about Afro-Carribean Spiritual Concepts, when he really surprised me and started talking about de ja vous and clairvoyance.

He started telling be how I had shut down my gifts, but these gifts were hereditary and that my daughter had inherited them. He went on to tell me that my nature was to kick nonsense aside as he made this motion with his foot. He explained that I could still recoup my gifts and somehow turned this very spiritual conversation into a warning about my wife and the games that she will plays in our marriage to assure that she gets the lion's share of our assets. He made sure not to say anything bad about her, but suggested that I needed to remember what she is capable of. He asked if I had a girl friend and I responded that I wasn't divorced. He suggested that I needed to have a woman that I can communicate with and explained that he was not talking about sex. I left his house wondering why this brief trip was turning into one massive conversation about my marriage.

I went to my counseling session and was given advise that my marriage may be too far gone to fix. I left the counselors office and dropped papers off at the house for her to set an appointment. I went from there to the home of another friend and sat with her parents for over an hour before Loretta came home. We talked for hours about Loretta's business plans and her new male friend. During the conversations she made the statement "Jacquie is the most purely selfish person I have ever known"! She went on the explain: "Sandra is selfish, but she will share, while Jacquie doesn't share with anyone. Jacquie called while we were talking and suggested that I stay at the house and go to the airport from there.

When I got there Jacquie was not home, so I decided to take a hot bath. When she got home I walked into the bedroom I asked why she had this strange look on her face? Her response was I could ask you the same question. She then proceeded to argue, but I have been through so many arguments I knew what to expect. As the argument progressed she started to threaten to call 911 to have me thrown out of her house. I suggested that she do so and since I did not fall for the bluff, she changed her approach and suggested that she did not have to call the police, because she had friends that would come and throw me out. Once again I suggested that she bring them on! Her arguments changed to how she wasn't going to have some White Psychiatrist, Lawyer, or Judge tell her what to do. She knows what she needs in her life and she needs God.

I suggested that she stop playing with God, because God is not stupid and knows when we are doing the right things. She responded I let the devil in when I let you through the front door of my house. She then went into her normal argument stating that I have a car and I can just leave. I explained to her that I did not come there to argue with her and after a continuous tirade I told her that she was going to continue with her lies and evil ways until she forces herself into the pits of hell. Now I don't know why I made such a statement, but the arguing ended abruptly.

As I fell asleep I recalled how on my previous visit she had made statements about my never having wanted anything. I had driven her to a favorite, fast-food burrito restaurant, because I sensed that she wanted something different to eat. We were driving past a group of apartments when I stated that the city had done an excellent job of remodeling. Her response was that I seemed to have an obsession with housing projects. I started to feel that everything that was happening now was some divine intervention. I have withstood the test and I am still strong and trying to do the right thing. I have done my penance and I am on the right road, but the lesson continued.

I got up the next morning, drove to the airport where I met two of my coworkers. I have known both of the ladies for over fifteen years, so Carolyn, whom I met first, suggested that I seemed full of anger. I assured her that I wasn't and that I was just feeling the impact of a negative encounter with my wife. We went on to discuss her sixteen year old son.

When Jeanne came to the podium she asked how Jacquie was doing. I explained that things were not going well and her response was: "I figured that"! She then asked if Nicole was my daughter, or my and Jacquie's Daughter. I explained that she was our daughter. She continued that she thought Nicky was Jacquie's step daughter, because she noticed that Nicole is so much closer to me than she is to Jacquie. As I entered the plane she advised "don't let her use her handicap to control you"! "You need to get on with your life.

I decided that it was time to contact one of our associates who is a trained psychologist and has known us, as a couple, for many years. Her daughters and Nicole grew together from elementary school and we have done many things together. She and Jacquie have maintained a semi distant relationship during the years that I have been in Maryland. Jacquie has told me that friends that are close to her don't see things as I do, but none of the people that she talks about know anything about me. I made a point of not asking questions, but opened myself to opinions from those who knew us as a couple.

Luisa really made a point of letting me know that she loved both of us, but that she and others never thought that our marriage would last. She expressed that her opinion was based on many years of working in a mental health environment and advised that she and many of our friends never understood how our marriage survived. When I asked if she thought Jacquie loved me, her response was, I believe she thinks she does, because you are a very gentle man. She went on to explain that she believed that the marriage stayed together because I loved Jacquie. She explained that Jacquie was not like us and that she thoroughly understood, because she worked with many people who reasoned as if they were in another dimension. She continued: "You need to realize that Some people just don't think like us"! She said that she had watched Nicole try to get approval from her mother, for years, and Jacquie always seemed intent upon destroying Nicole's self esteem.

I always liked Luisa, but never heard her speak like this. The fact is that I always thought of her as a little different, but special. Luisa is very sweet, caring, precious, sharing and unique. I left our conversation with a better understanding of how our associates saw us. I had heeded the words of the others that I talked to, but Luisa must have been thinking about the situation for many years; as had my sister in law. When I opened myself to receive information, I got what I needed, but not what I expected. Luisa stated clearly, You will have to end the relationship, because Jacquie does not want to lose her things and she has more things than anybody that I know! I discovered during that week that Luisa and many friends that I never expect to help, were there for me and Nicole.

My sister in law had opened her conversation with, I have waited years to tell you how I feel, but waited for you to ask! So, get ready for the bomb! Luisa simply told me how she felt and advised me that her perceptions were based on 25 years as a mental health professional, her training as a mental health employee and what she believed was my understanding of psychology.

I had a long talk with my brother about he and his wife and he suggested that he was not going to bring another woman into his life as long as he has school aged children, because she would have to be second to his children and no women should be subjected to that. He explained that he will stay with the mother of his children, even as his older children have suggested that they would support him, if he decided to move on. I knew how he felt, because I had waited for Nicole to finish high school. He explained to his wife that he needs his moral support and in talking to her I understands. She has baggage from early years and her relationship with her mother, so there are similarities between her mother and my wife. Conversations between she and Nicole benefitted both of them.

My sister has told the story about her relationship with her ex Husband, a Vietnam Veteran, who shot her five times when she finally decided to leave him. She explained how her mother in law and a preacher went to court and tried to lie to the judge and blame her for the problems in the marriage. The judge turned out to be smarter than anticipated and got him to confess what he had done. He was sentenced to a VA Hospital Ward for the mentally impaired, but his mother was able to get him released and married to another woman. I now realize that something in my past will not allow me to leave my children and that my siblings are similarly affected.

Luisa also resolved a major issue in our relationship, when she confided that Jacquie seemed to know how to pull the right strings and get things though she had so little education, or skills. She could not understand how Jacquie made so much money and reached the level that she had. I told her that it was through an EEO Lawsuit that she got her current position. That she had been terminated from her prior position and did not know what direction to take, so I chose a lawyer, read and explained all of the legal transcripts, worked two jobs and slept on the floor, in an empty room to save money to help pay the legal fees.

I have been denied so many jobs and growth opportunities so many times that I know the games by instinct. I also explained that Jacquie did not understand what had taken place, and that I got no credit once her lawsuit was resolved. When she got her settlement she responded as if I was a stranger and went back to her old ways. When one of her girlfriends tried to take credit for having found the attorney Jacquie thanked her, but the attorney just happened to be present and explained that it was through my and his association that he took her case. I fought the fight for her and she won, but as is usual, I lost in our relationship.

She loves things and could care less that her world is collapsing around her, that her health is going the way of her world, or that her husband and children are gone. I recently read a report stating that the government has changed bankruptcy laws such that one can no longer get a lot of credit cards, charge them to the max and file for bankruptcy. She has now lost a strategy that she and her girl friends revered.

Loretta, a family friend, explained that she had seen Jacquie's friends, at the social security office where she (Joanne) was trying to get the government to pay her house note. During their brief conversation Joanne complained about Jacquie's predicament and explained that Jacquie was angry about my divorcing her. Loretta says that she just listened and gave no response. Joanne also complained that she caught Jess in bed, at their home, with a White Woman, who claimed that he raped her. She also found out that he had a child by a Mexican Lady and the child was fourteen years old, so the affair happened during their married years. I knew that they would stay together, because her lifestyle was contingent on scams that he and she participated in as a team. Jacquie's choice of associates and her ability to get her siblings support in her unethical activities left me no choice!

I told Loretta that a lady that I worked with at Frontier Airlines had advised me, in 1984, to stay away from Jess and Joanne and I had taken her advise, because I respected her as a co worker. Over the years her advise proved to be valid, because Jess and Joanne filed more bankruptcies and insurance claims than all of my associates combined. I was concerned that either Jess, or Joanne would fake a fall on our property and sue us. Jacquie once complained that she was tired of Joanne taking advantage of her, but maintained a close association, because Joanne took sides against me.

Chapter 20

Attorney Cohn,

Please understand that perjury, is not a concern for Jacquie. She did not submit1997 tax forms, because she is getting two checks from her job. She did not submit information on profit sharing from her company, because she wants half of my retirement. She did not submit information on $68,000 from her most recent insurance scam, and our insurance man says she has made eleven claims, since I left Colorado. To quote her: "I will pay her for the rest of my life"!

She suggests that the furniture in a $250,000 house is worth $2,500, but the baby grand piano cost $8,000, the dining room set over $5,000, art collection and silver collection of is worth more than $2,500 individually. The sculpture, on the baby grand piano alone, is worth $2,500. I submitted photos of the living and dining rooms for your perusal. She also collected $25,000 from an EEO settlement, and earned over $20,000 in profit sharing. If you combine claims against Farmers and Aetna Insurances, it will become apparent that she is not submitting accurate information. She either, has forgotten that I know where the skeletons are, or she still thinks she is dealing with nice, honest, Bill! She often complained about my being too honest, but needs to realize that I am neither blind, nor stupid. The home was recently appraised at $250,000 and we owe $139,000.

She has filed another claim against Farmers and they want me to come to Colorado, so they can question me. The agent has suggested that he knows that I am not involved, but that they are afraid to go after her, because she is legally blind! He explained that she had Reggie, during a visit to Denver, bring all of the items into our dining room and place them on the table, so he could see them. She got a floater policy, and one year later, claimed the items in a burglary report. He says that he now realizes that it was all planned and wants to see her go down. He also explained that all claims were after I moved to Baltimore, but that Reggie was involved in the last effort.

A check with Aetna Insurance and the Westminster Police Department will show that many of the items were claimed when she filed a burglary report in 1984. "There has never been a burglary in that house". She broke the basement window when she got locked out, and when I was going to get it replaced she said that she would take care of it. A more efficient police department would have noticed that the door locks require keys to get inside and out and that neighbors on both

sides are home days, so how did someone move a truckload of items from that basement window without being noticed.

Respectfully
Bill

When Jacquie received checks totaling $68,000 from Farmer's Insurance she, flew to Baltimore, arriving at 3:15pm and left at 6pm. She exhibited no wifelike emotions, so I made up my mind that I had done all that I could to try to maintain the relationship. I signed the checks to hurry her on her way back to Denver, but I also made a decision that it was time to file for a divorce. She told my daughter, that during her brief stay, I treated her like a criminal: "If it walks like a duck"! My daughter suggested that she came to rub her success, in getting money from the insurance, in my face.

She tried to get her father to convince me to get involved in ripping of the insurance company, but I said no, and explained that only Jacquie benefits when she runs her scams. I spent many years arresting people for similar activities and Jacquie knew how I felt about what she was doing. The insurance investigators and lawyers tried to coerce me to come to Denver to verify the claim, but I know that I could go to jail, if they were not satisfied with the outcome. "That is the plight of being a "Black Man in America"! I received nothing from that claim and am not going to put myself in a situation that would endanger my efforts at getting Nicole through college. Reggie can be charged with helping her and he will not get any of her "Dirty Money" either.

The insurance company's hired guns (lawyers) wanted me to make a deposition, under oath and suggested, to our insurance agent, that I will tell the truth, to protect myself. I avoided going to Denver, because prior experiences have led me to conclude that I should trust neither Blacks, nor Whites who reside there. A lack of leadership in the White Community and a lack of spine among Blacks who serve as spokespersons, for the establishment imply that I would be better off letting the insurance company and Jacquie hammer out their differences. Jacquie would let me and Reggie go to jail for what she has done, and my experiences working in the justice system lead me to feel that they too often make the wrong decision. I have been advised that the homeowners policy will be canceled and that she can no longer play the teary eyed, blind women game on the agency, so let the gauntlet begin.

The insurance agent trashed her recent claim and I tried to explain, to her, that she was being set to take a fall, but she was confident that she could pull off another scam. The best way for me to solve my problems is to move away from her as I have! She left openings for me to cover myself, during divorce proceedings, because I know where the skeleton are: "Including those she has forgotten"! She told our daughter that I tried to get her arrested!

When I filed for the divorce she started showing how deranged she is. During police training, I was advised: "Do not get into arguments with the hippie's, drug dealers and pimps, because they believe what they are doing is right and you feel that what you are doing is right, so you are at an impasse before an argument begins"! Jacquie believes what she does is okay, so legality, or morality, are non issues, therefore, I should be supportive. My attorney asked me to let her handle the case in ways that are befitting of Jacquie's reality. She was advised, by some who knew us as a couple, that I have been too nice. "My daughter, listening on the phone, says "Amen"!

I felt that she was salvageable, but I was only slowing her down! I was the conscience she never had, so when I moved back to Baltimore she had a free hand and she dealt it with the venom of a viper. She took advantage of whomever, using health problems as a weapon, while playing her dramas like a musical instrument. Our insurance agent and TJ MAXX took the brunt of her efforts, but insurance is access to the most available cash. TJ Maxx, in Baltimore, arrested her for stealing, so she could not enter any of their stores for one year.

I received strange warnings from spiritual people who sensed that I was in some form of danger. A minister, during a phone call at the job, suggested that I needed to fill the gap, if I wanted my wife to go to heaven, but I didn't know her, and chose to think that she was simply a caller to a place of business. An employee suggested that she was getting even for a past life experience, and a written message from a psychic who was an associate of a fellow employee, after I changed work locations, also suggested that she and I were together in a past life and she is getting even, because my ethics caused her to lose status. I am a spiritual person and feel protected by guardian angels, but she is cold, dark, uncaring and devious, and I sense no good in her presence. She can't pull me to the dark side, but I realize that she is comfortable doing what she does.

She says that it was the sex that caused her to decide to be with me for all the years, and that she never had a climax until she met me. I believe she decided that I was on my way to being the kind of person that she wanted to be with since I was president of a small college, politically active and had a good education. She complained that she was confused as to why she always made more money, while I have more education and skills. She never accepted the fact that companies do credit checks when I am apply for professional positions, that she is two persons in EEO Filings, or that I always felt destined to run my own business. I had to put a stop to my political activities, because bankruptcies, shoplifting, and false insurance claims would be headline items, if I decided to do anything really noteworthy.

When she had problems and needed to write letters, or reports I was her resource, but as she always got better jobs, which caused an ongoing conflict, because she had this image of the male as the provider. My opinions, had little value and she responded to my ideals with arrogance, argument, self-righteousness and no regard for the effect that her attitude, or actions had on our children. She was rewarded by an unethical system that is concerned with maintaining status quo, and uses Black Females to meet statistics without concern for the impact that such actions have on families, or communities.

The solidarity among crazies is creating a barrier that is separating right thinking adults. Liars are getting the jobs, attention in the media and money, while being ugly, loud, profane, ill-mannered, immoral, high maintenance and low profile has so many rewards, in our society, that many of our youth have begun to honor profanity, violence, materialism and self hatred. Profanity goes in a child's ears and out his mouth, but parent's tendencies toward excessive materialism are leaving children to rear themselves and those small minds are open to a lot more than profanity. The beneficiaries of decadence don't give a damn, because they are getting bigger houses, expensive cars, fine clothes, hypertension ulcers and stress disorders. Children are responding to lack of discipline and insensitive parenting with a level of violence that is tearing at the nation's social fabric.

Chapter 21

Jacquie knew that going to a trained counselor would expose some very ugly secrets, so she was right in not going for treatment, but divorce also exposes ugly secrets. I defended my position by telling the truth. Attorneys refused to handle her case, because they realized that she was not being honest, so my attorney had to petition the court to keep an attorney in place to whom she would submit filings that were approved by the court. She says the attorneys were flaky and refused to accept the fact that they saw through her drama. My statements were accepted and the judge ruled against the maintenance payments she fought for, so my philosophy of taking the high road paid off. I was never concerned that a judge would give her all of the families assets, or that she could con him/her with innuendoes and half truths. The attorney who handled her paper work had to sue for his money.

I felt inclined to try to get Jacquie to understand why we can not be together, but I reflected over the years and many times that I tried to talk to her to get her to see that we were going in different directions. I think of the times spent with her siblings and their children and how I felt that the children were being taught the wrong values. She is mean and insensitive toward siblings, nieces and nephews, so I realized that I could do nothing more.

I have worked with pimps, prostitutes, drug dealers, prison inmates and every kind of misguided person and have known many who are into doing the wrong things to get what they want. Some had issues that ate away at their insides for years, and later surfaced in the form of declining health and early departure. Others ended up in jail, a half way house, or mental institution. Friends moved away from Jacquie and advised me that the time had come for me to move on. I was never alone, because "spiritually" friends and I came together. My eyes were opened and the time came when it was up to me to take charge and utilize the wisdom that was passed from grandma, my mother and all the women who gave me their DNA.

I can only hope that new associates who are trying to do the right thing will see Jacquie, to quote Tony, "For what she really is". I have rediscovered the family that I lost during my years with her and life has gotten better. In a new relationship, I inherited new in laws who are like me, and my daughter is benefitting. I was reared among women who were concerned and sharing and I am once again in that mix.

There are two clichés' that will guide me into the future and become an integral part of my mental processing, with any new partner. The first: "In a relationship, either both parties win, or nobody wins" and "Whatever you do to develop a relationship, you must do to maintain a relationship"! Jacquie stated that she felt that she was doing all of the work and preparation for our outings when we first met and doesn't remember having a good time. I responded that she should not have done those things, if she did not enjoy doing them, because those are the things that set the standard for our being together. If she had been honest, at the beginning, we could have bypassed a lot of difficult years, because I surely would not have spent all of those years in the marriage, if I had known that those first two years were not sincere efforts. She ultimately verified what I always felt: "That our relationship changed after we got married" and that none of our later years were like the first two.

The system is good to selfish people who have no conscience and a cadre of character flaws. When my daughter last talked to Jacquie's sister who moved to Atlanta and asked how she was doing. The aunt replied, "I'm blessed"! My daughter came to me and expressed her concerns that her aunt had no sense of right and wrong. How can anyone who lies, steals, and connives feel Blessed, and have the nerve to go to church on Sunday and feel safe?

I married a Jezebel, a Delilah, the biblical succubus, but thrive on the belief that a Just God doesn't give you burdens without reason. I am quick to tell my associates that Mrs. Delaney didn't raise any wimps and that my dad advised: "If it appears to be a wimp, kill it at birth"! I had to be strong, because this marriage challenged every standard I ever had. I am a one woman man, and, originally, decided that I would not get married again. I would remain a one woman man, let the woman keep her place, so she can go home when she feels like being ugly and I would go back to my place, if I feel like acting stupid. Hopeful, I was given me the wisdom to know when I am being difficult! This was not because I felt that all women are tainted, but because I didn't want to make the same mistake again. I knew that there were good women out there and that I would find one, but I also knew that I did not want to inflict my baggage on someone else.

Meanwhile, Jacquie, at divorce, was preparing for her next victim. She had my attorney change her middle name to Reggie's Dad's last name on the divorce papers! I knew that she has a second social security and probably felt that she can start over without the bankruptcies, insurance frauds and a shoplifting arrest. I asked my daughter if she had any ideas as to why she was going to use Reggie's Dad's name: "We both reached the same conclusion"!

During divorce proceedings Jacquie called and asked for favors, but I only asked one from her: "That she pay off the credit cards that were joint, so I could clear my credit, get our daughter a car and buy a house. Her response was that she wasn't going to do anything to help me. Earlier I made reference to a psychic reading from a friend of a co worker. I never met the psychic, but sent him a list of ten business questions that I wanted answered. It was answers that I did not ask for that surprised me. He gave me information that goes back to my relationship with my grandmother who passed away in 1958 and suggested that I needed to have a conversation with Jacquie with no lawyers present. Jacquie and I talked twice one day and I was surprised at our first conversation, since it appeared that she was listening to tapes that were helping her overcome her selfishness. A later conversation let me know that she was mimicking the words, but that she had not changed.

I suggested that I was probably the one person that she never listened to, and she responded, "I was grown when I met you and did not have to listen to you"! Prior to that statement I was thinking, "Maybe, there would be an opportunity that we could become friends and that our pasts would aid future spiritual growth". I suggested that we were supposed to be a team, that both sides should be heard and that it was not enough to listen, or read, but that she needed to learn. As she went on to tell me that I was not successful until I met her, I thought of one of her sister's husband and how he managed a Doggie Diner Restaurant and owned a Janitorial service before he met her. Jacquie said that he was nothing until he met her sister, but when he finally left her he was a broken man with serious health problems. He moved back south, where his family cared for him until his death. Is that what was in store for me, if I had gone along with her program!

The system worked against her in our divorce settlement and my attorney asked why I settled for so little once the judge gave his ruling that I was entitled to half of everything, including the insurance money. My philosophy is to always take the "high road" and not let her habits change who I am ! I am a one who stands by his principles and I refuse to change because of a few challenges in life.

The divorce made life easier for me and my credit was cleaned up instantly. I bought my daughter a car, bought a house, in Baltimore, and spent a week in Cancun with my daughter, my brother and his wife. We visited the Mayan Ruins at Chichen Itza and swam with the dolphins in Xel-Ha, rather than shop as we did on trips with Jacquie. I put my daughter's name on the mortgage, increased my insurance, made plans to send her to Europe and Africa, to close out her college education, and three of her cousins spent the summer with her, traveling between Baltimore and New York.

I brought Reggie's daughter's back to Baltimore and later took them to Los Angeles to hang out with my brothers children. My goal was to give them access to responsible and respectable adults, since I now have the freedom to do things such that the next generation will more readily handle challenges to an unfair system.

Chapter 22

In midsummer 1998 my daughter in law introduced me to a young lady that I thought I wanted to spend some time with. I have lived in Baltimore, since 1990 and Jacquie lives in Denver, so I started refusing telephone calls, because Jacquie and I have never been able to talk for more than a few minutes without arguing. This lady and I talked for hours, on the phone, so I concluded that our standards were compatible. She had divorced her husband, two years earlier, because he was sleeping around. She supposedly, had the good judgment to know that she could get S.T.D and decided to leave him regardless of her, or his financial predicament. That is the information that I was given initially, so I admired her for her stance and the love that she proclaimed for her son. We finally met on a warm sunny San Francisco Afternoon in September and while it was apparent, from our telephone conversations that she was a prize, when she exited the car I noticed her proud, long, legs. She spent most of that night in my arms and it felt good, but I was out of the loop for so long that I didn't anticipate my own responses. The next day I felt that she was with me, but her mind was elsewhere. "It was more like a one night stand"!

She suggested that she had to go to Sacramento to be with a sick Aunt, but would be back to see me off. She must have forgotten that I lived in the Bay Area for fifteen years and as President of a small college spent numerous hours in and out of Sacramento and knew the travel time between the two cities. She later explained that she had too much on her plate and needed time. She failed to explain a male friend who stopped and leered into the car as we were leaving my ex daughter in laws home. I knew that we, both, had to resolve conflict in our lives, before we could be together, but there were signs that I was not being told the truth. Often, after that night together, when I would say hmm and smile I was asked what I was thinking about. I usually responded: "It was a pleasant thought"!

I reacted to her age and good looks, but I knew that she stood to gain as much as I. She didn't take time to get to know me and I didn't get the opportunity to know her! Maybe she wasn't ready for change? I asked questions, but never got answers. One day I decided that I wanted a larger photo of her, so I took the negative to a local WalMart to have it developed. WalMart lost the negative, so I phoned and asked her to allow my daughter in law to copy her print and send the copy to me. We talked briefly, during which she explained that she was not angry and that she would comply. The following day she responded to my daughter in law: "That mo——Fu——asked me for his picture back"!

During a later trip to California to visit with Reggie's daughters, Tanya asked me to tell her male friend something that was not true. I am uncomfortable with lying and let her know that I was not interested in deceiving anyone, for any reason. As I am of the opinion that people who misstate facts are habitual at doing so, I started asking questions about why she introduced me to her friend and wanted to know what this friend was doing while her ex husband cheating on her. The response was, "She stayed with the same man for eight years until she found out that he was married to a White Woman". I suggested that: "They should have stayed together and maintained a business relationship"! "Why give up all that has been invested, if both are cheating"? Tanya agreed, but I kept wondering why she considered introducing me to a cheating friend. My experience with Californian's is that: "They don't consider the consequences of their actions and do what feels good at the moment".

We all played a part in the transition from respect to disrespect in our great nation. When I compare the consequences of relationships that are built on selfishness, falsehoods and material versus those built on caring and respect; caring and respect has always won, in the final analysis. My mother lost a good husband, ended up with a creep, then changed her value system. My sister says, she felt that after 40 she would not find a good man. My siblings and I feel that bad decisions cut many years off her life, while my grandmother and aunts who chose caring and respect lived well into their eighties and nineties. My mother was vibrant, educated and beautiful, but didn't make it out of her sixties. My daughter's Mother lives in a big house, in rural Texas, alone, with her material. She was alone for the last ten years of our marriage and will probably remain alone, because all of her choices are about money, material and a house: "The children and I were just along for the ride"! She has what she worked hardest to gain, but blames her being alone on me and her children I have sister in laws who believe that Delaney men are diamonds in the rough.

My mother and father loved each other all their lives and after over twenty years of separation, died only months apart. The approach I have taken is that I will fix my life rather than live the frustrated existence that is prevalent among so many who belong together, but will not do what is necessary to stay together. I want to be around those who are like me, so players, liars, cheaters and fools are off limits. I have good friends and family members that I enjoy spending time with. I ask questions, because I think that too often the heart and soul of some are MIA, but my sister in law says that I should thank Sheila for bringing me out of a twenty year rut.

I believe that women maintain their great looks, and their essence by eliminating bad habits and men who treat them badly. Tina Turner looks good at her age, because she had the guts to kick back when she got tired of Ike mistreating her, and Lena Horne looks good, because she realized that the Nicolas Brother that she married was no good and kicked him to the curb. Life is about making the right choices and decisions, but when we do otherwise we pay. A heart is as valuable as a brain, and if the two function together, life can be long and rewarding. However, when they operate unilaterally we miss much of what life is really about. My approach is to give my all and let my woman decide whether I am in her best interest.

I decided to proceed with caution and not take new relationships for granted. I spent time with my daughter, my sister, brother and their children and remained patient! My sister in law has wanted to introduce me to her idea of a good woman for many years and actually had a particular individual in mind. My nieces agree with the woman that she is thinking about, but my instincts say no and my brother suggests that they should not be matchmaking.

I communicated with a number of females and some suggested that I should start dating. I met a few who made me feel that I wanted to chance a relationship, but I decided to go to Roanoke and spend time with women that I knew during my early years. "Mary" has been my younger sister's best friend since third grade, so it seems that I have always known her and we had open and honest conversations about our lives. I was surprised at how much she knew about my family, so as we talked about things that I can't discuss with my sisters, I realized that she has been both observant and analytical. She caused me to remember things that I had forgotten and to discuss matters that I thought of as family secrets. We talked about ex spouses and agree that we had a lot of growing to do when we left our parent's homes.

We discussed siblings, parents, past loves, children, past relationships and where we are today, because of those relationships. I was so surprised at the depth of our discussion that I went over the conversations with my daughter, and spent the next few days pondering all that she knew about me, my family and how honest she was about herself and her family. We agreed that I would visit Roanoke more often, because this is where I can resolve my issues and eliminate psychological baggage that has cluttered my life. It had been a long time since I was been able to talk to a woman and feel that we can be friends, because we know who we are, what we are and what we want. I'm in no hurry. My encounter with Sheila proved to be disappointing and I felt as if I had met another Jacquie! I don't need another conniving, insensitive female in my life.

On my next visit we talked even more extensively, but the big surprise was when I was leaving to return to Baltimore. I spent four days in Minneapolis at my brother's, daughter's wedding and during that time was told, by one brother, Johnny, that Mary always had a crush on me. When my brother, Jacquez, and my sister, Jeanette, confirmed that same was true, they expressed disbelief that I never knew. After two days of talking Mary hugged me, at the door asked me to do her a favor and "Try to love her back"! I looked at her surprised as she asked me to "Please think about it"! I left thinking that I must have misunderstood her, but my daughter explained that she heard her and offered a number of ideas about how I needed to respond to her.

Nicole suggested that Mary was not looking for someone to do things, because it is the right thing to do, which she says is my way, and explained, that I should be cautious about how I respond to Mary. My daughter talked about women's feelings and explained how my words appeared flirtatious and encouraging. She suggested that my habit of flattering women could be damaging to Mary and that she noticed how Mary lit up when I put my arm around her as we walked into a book store. Mary explained, the following day, that I made her feel good when I caressed her as we entered the shopping mall. She felt that she was not dressed to her standards but I made her feel precious.

Nicole is insightful and sensitive and I am proud of where she is going with her life. Hopefully she will meet men who can do what Estelle and others have done for me. Maybe, just maybe, she will fall back with someone who knows who he really is and what he is all about and they will become good friends, or more than just friends. My daughter deserves it, but she does not deserve the strife and hardships Mary has experienced. If she learns from her parents and her past she will make better choices than, and that's what life is about: "Choices"! I can't teach her what a woman should know, because men and woman are different, but she is intuitive, traveled and learned. Her past is not my past, or her mothers past. She is the beginning of a generation that is better prepared than I and in tune with nephews and nieces who have been taught what my siblings have learned and taught.

Nicole and Mary were impressed with each other and Mary suggested that she should have been her daughter anyway. "I always thought that she should have been Estelle's Daughter". Estelle would have been a good mother and we would have stayed together, if we had a child, because my family trait is to stay with the children, regardless of head trips, or character flaws of our partners. Mary is a special person, but it was Estelle who gave me the love that carried me through the years. Maybe, Estelle prepared me for a re entrance into Mary's life at a time when we can both appreciate where we have been and where we can go in the future. I remember the lessons that I learned from Charlene, Angie, Eve, Jacquie and Sheila. Is Mary really ready for who I have become? I knew that I had to do better by her than I did by Estelle and I wanted to do the right thing, so I remained cautious, listened and learned. I have heard my daughter who has watched me, learned from me and made suggestions that make sense. I suppose it is time for the child to teach the father. She only wants the best for her dad, so how can I lose.

One lady who suggested that we date, before I talked to Mary, opened up and I became less than impressed. I suggested, to her, that I would start dating in 1999 and I am glad I waited, because I, now, more easily recognize her attitude about travel and religion. Statements such as: "I am not going outside this country with all those crazy people", suggest that we are from two different worlds! Religious conversations are even more telling and I am not one to get caught up in a particular belief system such that I will stop growing emotionally, spiritually, or intellectually. One who competes with God for the heart of a partner is foolish and entering a competition that he, or she is guaranteed to lose. Spirituality usually enhances a relationship, but religious zeal and a closed mind are deadly companions. Any woman who enters my space must be willing to grow beyond her parents and into a world that is continually evolving. I will not go backward, except to review and aid future growth. My past, present, and future will be part of a process that will continue to bring together all that I learn as I travel through life.

One of my co worker's introduced me to a lady from his homeland, The Philippines, and I felt that she was more like me, than most of the African American Women that I considered. She is staunch Catholic, but as spiritual as she is religious. She suggested that she asked God to send her a good man and I sense her relationship with her God, as compared to one in which she simply follows the dictates set by her parents. She is considerate, has the benefit of a good education, understands my relationship with my daughter and has a similar relationship with four sons. She was widowed for over ten years, is observant, appreciative, patient, has a good business mind and is loyal, almost to a fault. My effort is not to be self centered and inconsiderate while trying to learn about her and her culture.

I sense a natural bond, but wanted to be cautious. I have much to learn and as I know what I am about, I need to be sure that I am not overbearing. She is five feet, one inch at 112 pounds, while I am five feet, eleven inches and weigh 200 pounds, so I need to make sure that she is comfortable when we are alone. We went on dates and gatherings with her family and friends, and I asked her to go to Los Angeles with me to meet my brother and sister in law. I wanted to be sure that she was comfortable with our sleeping situation, because she did not believe in sex before marriage, which was okay by me. I asked questions about her life with her husband and whether she did her man's bidding and had sex to bear children, versus as an enjoyable part of a complete, wholesome relationship. She answered all of my hard question and told me when she was embarrassed by my requests for information.

I want to do what makes my woman happy, so we have a lot of talking to do. I also want a travel and business partner, because I feel that I have a lot more living to do. I explained that I have to start rebuilding, because I did not want dirty money from Jacquie to burden my karma. I have the opportunity to make money and do not want negative energy in my life. My approach is not to get caught up in unethical habits.

Edita was to go back to the Philippines in February of 2000, but my plans were that I would not let her get that far away, because I have met no one as uniquely considerate as she, since Estelle. I considered marrying her at a local courthouse and observing her religious and cultural practices until we were sure that we wanted to be together. She would remain with her sister and brother in law and, if things work out we can marry in a Catholic Service, after which we will consummate our marriage. I married Estelle in a Catholic Service and God was good, to us, for the five years that we spent together. Maybe, I have learned and am prepared to run the final gauntlet.

She is much like Estelle and a step above other women that I have known. As I watch her, I am assured that I was correct in being overly cautious with other women. I knew what I didn't want, but was not sure about what I needed, because my second wife appeared to be a good choice for two years, and changed after we wed. She mimicked my ideals, but went back to being her natural self once we said "I do"! I found myself referring to Sheila as "Sibyl", because, like Jacquie, she never gave straight answers, and I realized that Mary, like many Black Females, has a chip on her shoulder.

Things, suddenly, became crystal clear! I want a woman who is honest, trusting, open, tender, caring, and whose love has no boundaries. She must be a team player and able to understand that I am looking to do things different than my parents and ancestors. I will not trust others to control my destiny, but realize that I have the responsibility of managing an honorable, loving relationship. When Edita professed her love for me, I quickly realized that I had been here before, with Estelle, and had mishandled our love! Now, I am being given a second chance, a reprieve, but this time my ideas and ideals are intact. I have been lucky, but at this juncture in life I am skilled, know who I am and what I must do, so I will not fail. She will benefit from my experiences and travels and I will benefit from her culture and standards, but to fail twice is not my way. I made a promise to Edita and myself and I will keep that promise. She will always be first, on my agenda and I will honor and respect her "Till death do us part"! I was taught life's lesson by a "Queen B", but memories of my mother, grandmother, many aunts, sisters and Estelle, will guide me toward a pleasant future!

Chapter 23

THE FINE ART OF DISCRIMINATING

Earl Nightingale (Nightingale-Conant) in his speech "Strangest Secrets" says: "The mind is like a fertile field. If you took two pieces of land and in one you planted corn to feed the masses, and in the other you planted nightshade, which is deadly poison, earth will produce corn and nightshade in equal abundance. Likewise, the mind will produce negative and positive in equal abundance!"

There can be great lessons in adversity, if one is willing to open his mind and learn. I spent my life living up to a philosophy of taking the high road and not attempting to benefit using unethical, or immoral means, while many tried to taint my image. In the Air force, it was unethical, incompetent, racist non commissioned officers, and during my law enforcement years it was frightened, racist managers, but my selfish, unethical spouse was the strongest barrier against my efforts to succeed". Challenges from those that you are supposed to be able to trust and, who, at times, prepare your food and warm your bed are the most debilitating.

She had credit cards, in my name that she refused to pay, filed bankruptcies, committed insurance fraud and was arrested for shoplifting, which made it very difficult for me to be politically active, apply for business loans, or professional jobs. I knew that insurance investigators would just as well send me, or my son to jail to close their books, so I stayed in contact to assure that the onus remained in her corner. She says that I tried to have her put in jail, but I was simply covering my rear, while Reggie never realized that they were looking at him: "I wanted to keep it that way"! He has enough to deal with! I tried to explain that a spouse's ethics and personal finances are taken into considered in most endeavors outside our home, but she never got the message. She could care less about other than herself, so she minimized all efforts to level the economic playing field, for me, and the children.

There is ample evidence that African Americans must develop new approaches to dealing with this capitalist democracy, if we are to survive and prosper. Many of us have worked hard and long to educate ourselves and do those things that we have been told are the right things to do to become viable, but we still find ourselves on the outside looking in. We train many who are less competent for jobs that we are never offered, and watch as doors of opportunity open to those who are without skills, or experience, while we are not even allowed in the waiting room. Upon coming home, our spouses ask what we did wrong, when it was what we did right that was our downfall.

The real challenge is to parlay our experiences to our children, while developing a game plan such that they will enter the skirmish armed with information, intelligence and financing and prepared to fight the better fight. This task is made difficult by the fact that wise children have seen our plight and know that the path is booby trapped and treacherous. Many have decided to achieve in the way that many Europeans built wealth and power.

I decided, early in life that I would proceed in such a manner that I would not suffer the anguish that my father, uncles and associates experienced. I listened to stories told by my parents, my elder relatives and their friends and decided that life would be different for my children. My father said: "Whatever you do in life, you attach your signature and it reflects what you think of yourself. He continued: "Anything worth doing is worth doing well"! In the world outside my family, ethics and standards proved very different.

In June 1960, while home on leave from basic training and en route to Europe, I was arrested for drunk, disorderly conduct and harassing White Females. It didn't matter that I didn't drink, smoke, or consume illegal substances, and there were no White females in this "Black Community". Those who came to court to support the White Male who accused me were "Black", had known me, since early childhood, and still they supported his claim that I had harassed him, and his customers, for the past three to four months. What they didn't know was, that I had been at Lackland Air Force Base in Texas, for six months and had arrived in town less than twelve hours earlier. Imagine their shock, when Mom and a "White Police Officer" presented copies of my military orders to the judge.

The system never had a chance to abuse me, because my support started at home, my parents were there for me, and I have been lucky enough to know some good people. My parents were tough, intolerant and always said: "I hate a liar and a thief and if you will lie, you will steal"! They kicked ass, but I learned, early, that I could avoid getting whipped by doing the right things. Those early experiences and that "White Police Officer"caused me to be caring, sensitive and a pain to those who used the system for unethical purposes, when I became a San Francisco Police Officer.

In 1969, while working to provide a service to my community, I was charged with un-officer like conduct by the S. F. P. D., because I threw some cards, that turned out to be PSA Airline tickets, in the garbage. They had been placed in my mailbox with a note stating: "Take your Hunters Point Buddies to the San Diego Zoo", so I thought that it was just another racist joke. At no time did the media report the situation as it happened, but bits of truth were at the end of articles, because it is known, among media employees, that most readers only read the first paragraphs. The concept is called pyramiding and the important information is supposedly placed at the beginning of stories. The cards had no names, so I had no idea that they had value until three days after I threw them away and was asked by Sergeant Simmons whether I had gotten the cards. I was advised to check the trash which was emptied daily. Somehow four were still in the trash receptacle, so I was told to check to see whether they were any good. During this time in my life, I received thousands of dollars in donation for projects that I was involved in, and I worked long, hard hours, so I sent them to PSA with a note requesting: "If they have value, that any monies be donated to The Hunters Point Festival which I work with, but do not handle funds for".

My greatest concern, is that I blamed Sergeant Simmons for setting the scam in motion, when he may not have been involved. He took the brunt of racial problems that came into the unit, because we were divided along racial lines and he was, to Blacks, the more conservative of two sergeants. The other was nothing to write home about but the big disappointment was our Lieutenant, because he was an instructor at City College and failed to perform up to standards we discussed in class. I believe that the individual who put the tickets in my mailbox was Black and what I refer to as a "Go along to get along, House Negro, and only interested in self. Years later a friend from that era, who says he worked with the CIA, explained that this same Black Officer was a mole for the F.B.I., and assigned to work for him. I now understood why he was given a high salaried position in federal government, that was contrary to what most of us felt about his intellectual capacity. He was not the first, nor the last, of many who rose beyond their actual ability by lying on associates.

I was suspended, with pay, and never challenged the decision, because I was too busy, with more important issues to play cat and mouse with an insensitive police department. Still, San Francisco was years ahead of most departments, and my time there benefitted my social, political, spiritual and intellectual growth. Thirteen years later I ran for sheriff in Colorado and the article reappeared, so I was interviewed by a newsman from the Denver Post. Two days before election the Post printed their version of the story with innuendos in the first paragraphs and bits of truth near the end. Prior to this article, citizens who read both the Rocky Mountain News and Post, were probably thinking I was two different persons.

Photos printed by the Post were unflattering and made me look more like an inmate than an N.C.O. wearing military fatigues, while teaching a Primary Leadership Course to an Engineering Battalion for the U.S. Army Reserve School. My campaign chairman contacted the S. F. P. D., and was advised that in1982 they would have handled the case different than they did in 1969. The S.F.P.D. avoided legal altercations by stating that I served honorably and that in 1969 I could have been charged with un officer like conduct for something as simple as a button missing from my uniform jacket.

Meanwhile, The incumbent was concerned that our names would get people mixed up, because "Delaney" sounds White and "Johnson"sounds more like the "Black Guy". He made claims that I was not qualified to be his desk sergeant, while his only law enforcement experience was three years as a deputy in tiny Emporia, Kansas, and a high school diploma. I had military police, campus, and S.F.P.D. experience, an Advanced P.O.S.T. Certificate and California Certification to teach Police Science at the Community College Level.

I ask for "No special consideration", because I believe that "Life gets better as we get better"! Teddy Pendergrast sings in one of his songs: "The world won't get no better, if we just let it be. We gotta change it y'all, you and me"! In most cases we get ridiculed when we offer solutions that are better than our "White Bosses", and we must know that our fight often begins in our bedrooms, rather than in boardrooms. All information on the planet is minimized, if there is no unity in our families, and parents must mentor offspring and be attentive to peer and media influence that is designed to alter our course, and teach us to disrespect other Blacks.

Some Blacks have learned, through media, and "White Associates Influence" to criticize minority businesses for being high priced, or slow in providing services, so when I purchased my home in Baltimore, I heard the negatives that inner city residents hear from Blacks, who feel that they have escaped to "Vanilla Suburbs". They justify complaints, by talking about high taxes in the city, also learned from the media, while failing to calculate the price of homes in the suburbs versus the cost of paying taxes. Math is an exact science and put simply: "It costs less to live in the city"! When I tried to get a home improvement loan, businessmen from the suburbs were charging high prices for a small jobs, while inner city businessmen did not have access to capitol! In some cases, unethical Blacks front for Whites who take advantage of the system, and those same Blacks will do whatever is necessary to live down to the standards of "Admired" White Associates.

As an extreme example, American Media spent two years beating up O.J. for allegedly killing two "White's" and the effort continued after he was found "Not Guilty". This trial divided Blacks along racial lines, so Blacks who tend to accept White Values argue that the evidence that was presented was valid. They also argue, along with insensitive Whites, that the court did not allow the evidence that pointed to O. J. as the killer, and that O.J., in front of all those intelligent White Folks, spread his fingers, so the glove didn't fit. My law enforcement associates feel, as I do, that it was the blood evidence that makes the case unbelievable, but we know, based on experience, that the system invalidates Blacks who are brighter, or more experienced than acceptable norms, so our conclusions are "Naturally" wrong. The concept about incompetence of African Americans is also supported by go along to get along Blacks!

My brother Walter, a retired sheriff in Roanoke County, Virginia, was considered the genius in our well educated family and proved many cases for his department using sheer wit, to the dismay of White Counterparts, so his success made him unacceptable and limited his promotion opportunities. Harold Banks is a retired, college educated, detective from the Palo Alto, California P. D., was a Green Beret in the army, studied martial arts from karate to samarui and is adept with a knife, or sword. Harold encountered problems similar to Walter's in Virginia and what I dealt with in San Francisco. The better we became at our jobs, the more problems we had with our departments, butt we, still, have the gall to think that we have interesting summations about the O.J. Trial.

Harold talks about having to stop O.J. from bullying Marguerite when we were campus policemen at City College in San Francisco, so we concluded that Marguerite testified that O.J. never abused her to get even with Nicole for coming after O.J. while they were married. Our conversations go along the same lines as when we talk to most law enforcement professionals and against the reasoning of those who have no experience, insight, or training, but have been convinced by the media. We talk about the small amount of blood, the effort required to kill two people with a knife, collection, protection and dissemination of evidence, M.O. and all the things that law enforcement people talk about when in conversation among those who really understand. Harold and I were classmates of O.J., and have difficulty believing that the guy that we called "O.J. Simpleton" has the mental skills to do all that he is accused of doing, get rid of bloody clothes, and get back to his home and to the airport in the amount of time the prosecution projected. Hell, even after a shower, proper tests would have shown blood protein on his person, so who did the media really fool? The only difference between a good crook and some policemen is brains and guts. The average policemen is a nice, middle class foot soldier who is expected to work with groups that he has not been socialized to understand.

"Have you ever known a pre trial situation where the Black Man was "Not Guilty"! "The rule of law for Black and Hispanic Men in America is: "Guilty" until proven "Guilty" by a court of law!" That's why "Ethnic Profiling"is acceptable, and the Florida Sheriff who developed "Operation Pipeline",the grandfather of ethnic profiling, was able to get a "House

Negro" to speak up for his program, just as Republicans were able to get a "Sacramento, California House Negro" who is married to a "White Woman" to challenge "Affirmative Action"! Some Blacks and Hispanics still don't believe that "Driving while Black", or "Driving while Hispanic", is a reality. Can we guide children, when we are not sensitive to social issues that are in our faces every day of our lives?

I am not convinced of O.J's guilt, because my police training suggests the evidence was nonsense, and I suggest to some who are so sure of his guilt, that one needs a social consciousness to see how the criminal justice system really works. We can't forget lynchings and the many Blacks who have gone to jail, when some of us knew that they were innocent, just because it might harm our social status: "Our children are at risk"! Remember Hayward Patterson and the Scotts borough Boys, that one of the two white Girls admitted that she was not raped, and that "Patterson had syphilis". When Derek Jeter' co workers, both Black and White, stated that he was at work when the crime was committed, he was still convicted, and there are similar examples that suggest, to a reasonable mind, that we have problems in our system of injustice.

Had O.J. been found guilty would the justice system have put forth effort to correct the improper use of DNA, or the "Nonsense" that is prevalent when the fate of minorities, or the unempowered is at hand. Many who believe that O.J. was guilty are of the same ilk as those who saw Rodney King being aggressive toward the L. A. Policemen. Evidence that was presented suggests that Nicole and Ron did whatever O.J's 50 plus year old, ex pro football limbs wanted "Without a Struggle", and what difference did it make whether O.J owned Bruno "Ugly" shoes, since no shoes were presented as evidence. "The gloves didn't fit, the drops of blood on the door of the Bronco, the socks, the glove and inside his home, were not consistent with the volume of blood that is normally associated with a violent murder. Where is Ovid Demaris when we need him? He explained the Italian Rope Trick, In His Book "Last Mafioso", and we now need him to explain a "Colombian Necktie" to people who don't have a clue, but are convinced that they understand what happened at that crime scene. No one person committed that crime!

When did we start judging the time of death by a barking dog. My neighbor's dogs bark all the time, so should I to presume that people are being murdered. L.A. has a coroners office, so tell me what time the murder was committed, based on medical and scientific specifics. Dr. Lee was right! Something was wrong with blood evidence that was presented, and testifying officers put less effort into the handling of O.J.'s Blood than I took in handling a bag of weed. If I had the bad judgment to carry narcotics evidence around for three days, every case I submitted would have been thrown out of court, and San Francisco would have probably kicked me off the force. Unfortunately, the same actions by White Officers go unnoticed!

If some, who are convinced that they know what actually happened, became more involved in the justice system, they would be very afraid of the possibilities for themselves and their families. The only persons who can say "Positively" that the system works are "George Bush",during his stint as Governor of Texas, "The Ramparts Division of the L. A. P. D.", "The New York Policemen who fired forty one bullets at Diallo, the officer who stuck a broomstick up an detainee's rear, African American Females who were on the jury that freed the New York City Policemen, the jury that found in favor of the Los Angeles Policemen in the Rodney King Beating, Safe Negroes, P.W.T. and others who are socially, intellectually and morally unconscious.

I am a few years older than O.J., not damaged by pro football, throw very heavy bags across the bin of some very large planes, a member of Bally's Health Clubs, since 1967 and can make as good an exercise video as any former athlete, because exercises and luggage, don't fight back. A recent report, supposedly from O.J's current girl friend, say that she is afraid that he will kill her, but in the same article she says that he can hardly walk after a golf outing, because his knees are swollen, he has a huge lump on his back and may not live another three years. A week later

I read the same article, in another periodical, but without information about his knees and the lump on his back. Those of us who followed O.J's football career know his physical condition, and that his knees are the reason the Forty Niners cut him from the roster. Some of you need to stop looking at Sylvester Stallone Movies until you can realize that they are just movies, and that the media sells B.S. to the socially inept and some whose minds haven't develop beyond birth!

The O.J. Case caused the L.A.P.D. and F.B.I. Crime Labs to change the way they handle DNA, and 76 "Death Row Inmates" have been released from prison, because the correct usage proved that they were not guilty. During my criminal justice training, in college, and at the San Francisco Police Academy we were taught to operate on the premise that: "We would rather let a hundred guilty go free than imprison one innocent citizen"! Thanks to the improper use of DNA in the O.J. case and the expert testimony of Dr. Lee, others are finding that we have a history of convicting innocent citizens. Some of us already knew, but we also know that most Americans don't give a damn until they, or a loved one is impacted.

O.J., Al Cowens and I were classmates at City College at San Francisco where we studied Criminal Justice, while I served as a San Francisco Police Officer. O.J. went to U.S.C. to play football and I went on to San Francisco State where I majored in Developmental Psychology, because I wanted to understand why there were so many dysfunctional parents in my patrol district. Many of my former classmates chose the Black Panther Party over law enforcement, because we found little effort, by instructors, to live up to standards that were taught in the classroom, and instructors proved to be just as insensitive in real life situations. Experiences as a functioning police officer were even more distressing. Harold Banks, was our best and most experienced campus police officer, but happened to be Black, so when he applied for Chief of Campus Police, at City College he was given a position of captain without the authority to do his job. The Chief Position was given to a less competent White Student, and that is the way it has been throughout my employment experience.

I moved to Texas with plans to attend S.M.U's. Law School, but changed my mind, when Dallas' D. A. gave a presentation on how to keep minorities and females off juries. I attended grad school at the University of Texas at Arlington where I majored in criminal justice and urban affairs, but left when it was suggested, by a member of the Justice Department that I was unemployable, because Texan's, including Blacks, were unaccustomed to "Strong Black Male Images"!

Unfair decisions by college and police administrators, life experiences and the ability to read and understand the racist literature of the era sent me and my classmates scattering for answers that were not easily found. It was, however, abundantly clear that those who are in power use outright "B.S." to divide those who are uninformed, unwilling to learn and powerless to offer a legitimate challenge to a system that is hell bent on maintaining the status quo. O.J. was part of the group, in that he studied criminal justice, and was an athlete, but it is apparent that, after all he has been through, he has not learned.

Geraldo talked about O.J. on his daytime talk show, and later, used his night show to continue the charade, while supporting the thesis of a drug abusing "supposed" friend of Nicole's. Good old boy wannabee Geraldo went to San Francisco to get people who knew O.J.: " and got Lefty Gordon from the Western Addition's Booker T. Washington Center, while a more likely person would have been John Greenberg from Potrero Hill Recreation Center, since O.J. grew up in Potrero Hill! Was he afraid that people who really knew O.J. might destroy his crusade?

The Black Male is too often portrayed as violent, uncaring, selfish, irresponsible and incorrigible, so it was okay for the media to sacrifice Jon Benet Ramsey, the 168 family members who were killed in Oklahoma City and those who were maimed by the unabomber to crucify the image of "Ole Black Ass O.J.! Why not go all the way and claim that he was a member of the Aryan Race, KKK, Skinheads, Minutemen, Tax Protesters, Branch Davidians, and some local law enforcement offices, that have been a cancer in the national fabric for decades. Make him a CIA Employee and say that he sold weapons and drugs that helped the world's terrorist. Shucks, he had to be on the U.S. Military Base where Saddam Hussein was trained, and of course, he taught Jim Jones how to make "Poison Kool Aid, Jeffrey Daumer how to season meats", and Wasn't he a supporter of The Shah of Iran, Noriega, Marcos, Castro and Allende until they were no longer useful?

How could the media miss an opportunity to tie such violence to a "Black Man"! Imagine how many more uninformed Americans can be subjugated, then we can do business as usual and give more high profile positions to "Safe Negroes" and "Go Along to Get Along Whites" who help vilify minority males, such that we don't make the mistakes we made by not completely destroying the images of O.J., Michael Jackson, Ron Karenga, Jim Brown, Muhammad Ali, former Lieutenant Governors George Brown of Colorado and Merv Dymally of California, former congressmen Gus Savage, Adam Clayton Powell,......Do I see a trend here? How many "Safe Negroes" would get upset if I added Louis Farrakhan and Malcolm X to that list.

England could have put their two cents in and claim that O.J. helped the British Military train Idi Amin, but they did something much worse! The country that abolished slavery in the 12th century is now saying that the L.A.P.D., in it's effort to convict O.J., overlooked a key suspect: "Jason"! I can remember going into court, as a police officer, with proof that "Three Black Males" had been unjustly detained, to find that the judge didn't give a damn. Californian's System went overboard to free the policemen who were taped beating Rodney King, and New York did a better job freeing four policemen who fired forty one shots at an unarmed African. After one shooting, Mayor Juliana tried to prove that the shooting was justified by opening an expunged record of the victim, which allowed concerned citizens to prove that the police officer's criminal record was worse than the victims. Later we find that The N Y P D has also terrorized military intelligence officers.

There are many factors that impact relationships within minority families, and while many claim to be insightful, actions imply a different conclusion. When the question of whether Blacks still face discrimination is asked, most Whites say no and 34% of Blacks agree. I don't expect the opinion of Whites to change, but I wonder what closet the Blacks are living in. The Discovery Channel did a study and found that 79 percent of Whites and 42 percent of Blacks are biased in favor of White Ideals. If we have no vision of right and wrong, or the larger view of the universe, what can we teach children, after all is said and done: "You cannot teach what you do not know"?

Military Police, Campus Police, San Francisco Police Department, certification to teach Police Science in California's Community Colleges and my college training in behavior modification and social learning theory left me with one conclusion: "O.J. was Sleeping with the enemy"! "My ex is African American and I was "Sleeping with the enemy"! Discrimination is a factor impeding the progress of those who have no economic, or political clout, but nothing is more deadly than being romantically involved with a partner whose only interests are image and material. The ultimate impact of the Queen B's influence is on relationship outside our homes, and "Playa's", or "Queen B's" usually have no sense of destiny, purpose, or the world around them. They don't care how they affect other humans, and go through life like unattached wheels, when they are not too bright, but like unguided missiles when blessed with the gift of intelligence.

Analyze the difference between Little Kim, Snoop Doggy Dog, Lauren Hill and Will Smith, and between Gloria Allred, Nicole Brown's Sister, Ron Goldman's Father and Bill Cosby, and maybe you will get my drift. If you don't, you may need to ask yourself some real serious questions about your level of social consciousness. Lauren Hill, Will Smith and Bill Cosby's actions should make us proud, because of their personal stature and air of integrity. O.J. was guilty before he ever entered that courtroom and that is the way it has always been with Black on White crime situations. Whites have raped, maimed, lynched and found Blacks guilty of crimes that were committed when we were hundreds of miles away. One must be proud of self to project an air of integrity, because "What you do reflects what you are"!

Chapter 24

Whites, who don't care to hear the truth, say: "All Blacks talk about is "Race", while some need to say: "I am getting K.I.T.A.'s (kicks in the ass) too"! My response to this group is: "If someone is kicking your butt and you are tolerating it, that is your problem and you have to either stop them, or wear butt pads. However, to fail to recognize that Blacks and Hispanics are still being treated harshly is unacceptable"! If you are getting K.I.T.A.'s from a system in which you are considered an outsider, and coming home to a partner who is treating you even worse, you are in deep do do! No one can inflict more damage on your efforts to succeed, or load heavier psychological baggage on your children than your significant other.

Double jeopardy is when you are being tried twice for the same crime, but getting mistreated at home, on the job, among friends and associates, and other predicaments that are necessary to your survival is a life sentence of jeopardy. Discrimination is an art form for spineless individuals who fear honest competition and use society's ism's to get ahead! We need to face the reality that our youth have been infected and have internalized decades of innuendoes, hate, lies, disrespect and insensitivity, and have found new ways to release pent up anger. Consequences for White Youths have appeared in the media in Colorado; Arkansas, Oregon, Kentucky,.... while we still overlook actions against ethnic minorities. George Bush could justify his stance on the death penalty in Texas, because most of those executed are minority, but Whites who drug a Black Male behind a truck separating his head and shoulder from his body got life in prison.

Minority Youths expose their frustrations in ways that are different from White youths, because minority hate is internalized, while White Hate is "historically" external. Dr. Carl Bell a Clinical Psychiatrist from Chicago talks about "White Male Entitlement Dysfunction" stating "They think they own people and that's why they take everybody out with them"! I have known White Police Officers who felt that they have the inalienable right to kick the s—out of a perp, or plant drugs on those they want to charge with a crime. Many carry "Throw Down Weapons" in case they decide that they need to, or they accidentally shoot someone. Why become a police officer, if you can't respect the law? The harsh truth is, "In the good old U.S. of A the most important thing, is getting paid".

I watched White Male Students at the University of Colorado at Boulder sing "Jesus loves the White Man's Penis, to the tune of "Jesus loves the little children", and concluded "That's why they don't wash their hands" after going to the bathroom. Dr. James T. Reese a Clinical Psychologist and former FBI Profiler who consults Fortune 500 companies explains: "Today, the average White Middle Class Male has no sense of accountability for his behavior. The basic code is, if it feels good, do it, and now minorities are developing a similar attitude!

Dr. Julia Hare, a noted clinical psychologist with the Black Think Tank in San Francisco, states "Blacks and Whites express retribution differently. "Blacks seek out the individual, but when Whites went after Saddam Hussein, look at the innocent people they killed". Dr. Bell and Dr. Hare expressed concerns that Blacks will mimic White behavior as we try to assimilate into society. As I drive the streets of Baltimore, I have noticed that young "Black" Males act as if they own the road, and many of the Black Males that I work with do what feels good without concern for others. The shootings remind me of a John Wayne Movies, so Dr. Hare and Dr. Bell "We are already there"! "We need to face the fact that hate and disrespect are equal opportunity debilitators, and that we are mentors to a generation of spoiled, untended, misdirected, un disciplined children".

Some tried to developed game plans and took the courses, once we saw the handwriting on the wall. I took child psychology courses, worked with San Francisco State's Child study center and Sonoma State Hospital's unit for self destructive children. I also worked with the San Quentin Squires and California's Youth Authority, because I wanted to get a feel for the result of children being reared in so many un insightful predicaments. When comparing the children of rich parents with those of middle class and poor families one quickly realizes that the only difference is money, and children are undervalued in all segments of our society. If they weren't we would put more effort into realizing that parenting is a skill that can be learned, and "Children are a blessing"!

We need to stop looking at other's faults and fix ourselves. In recently conversation with a White Female who suggested that "Blacks are as prejudice as Whites": I responded: "We are remembering not prejudging, and we are still experiencing the wrath of those who fear that we will try to get even for the past". The 16th through 19th century, Rodney King, New York policemen in the Bronx, the Rampart Division of Los Angeles' Police Department and my current employer have a lot in common. I had as many negative experiences in the 1990's as I had in the 1960's", but I have changed. Those who have power want me in useless debate over nonsense issues, hoping that it will take my mind off the prize, but I am capable of issuing a challenge, aware of racial sociology and the mind games that exist in the business community, law enforcement and the media. I know that some Whites are abused and have not yet realized that those who are in power don't care about Poor Blacks, or Poor Whites, but I will not get caught up in isms' that keep some from viewing the big picture. If those with small minds want to waste time wondering who is most partial among others with small minds, let them do so. I have neither the time, nor the energy to waste, because I concentrate on the "Big Fish", the "Puppet Master"!

The debate is useless among those who have no desire to influence change. Whites are abused, because they haven't learned that insight is more valuable than hindsight. And for Whites who play the "Two wrongs don't make a right, so I am against quotas game", try working on a solution and get off the: "That was before my time B.S"! If you are not part of the solution, you are part of the problem.

Chapter 25

Do you remember the misstatements of Schockley and Jensen, in the 70's, or the conclusions in the book titled: "The Bell Curve"! Well the August 3, 1998 issue of Fortune Magazine exposed the fact that the fifty best companies for Blacks, Hispanics and Asians outperformed the S&P 500 over a three and five year cycle. Fifty of five hundred is a better statistical indicator than random samplings that are used to validate theories put forth by most social scientists. Isn't our capitalist democracy "Supposedly" designed to promote the best and the brightest. Well, fifty companies did just that and the outcome suggests a clear and present danger to companies that fail to do likewise. Recent studies imply that Middle America, where there are fewer ethnic minorities, will experience slower economic growth in the next millenium

Those of us who are aware understand that D.C. re elected Marion Barry, because we tired of double standards. White Politicians lie, steal, cheat, use drugs, sexually abuse women and children, sign of on illegal deals and control others using innuendos, but we don't spend millions of dollars to expose them. Denver, Seattle and Minneapolis are proud to have elected Colored Mayors who do what Whites want, and New Yorkers are too simple minded to realize that Juliani is a modern day Mussolini. Philadelphia Elected Rizzo Mayor after he terrorized the poor and minorities as Chief of Police.

In a city that is over sixty percent African American we chose in O' Malley, the best and brightest of three candidates, and refused to elect the lesser of evils. We heard claims that he split the vote between Black Candidates, that he wouldn't solve our education and drug problems, and all the rhetoric that comes with a political campaign, but we are smarter than that! All I ask of a politician is that he provide equal opportunity for me to feed my family utilizing skills that I have developed: "The rest is up to me"!

Unlike many scholars, I have no problem with theories put forth by "The Bell Curve" and believe that life regresses toward the mean. I have worked with many incompetent, uneducated, unethical, lazy Whites during my work years and understand that some Whites Managers only feel comfort when they promote non threatening minorities. Other Whites need to pull their head from their rectums, stop externalizing hate and recognize that incompetent management will not promote those who are smarter, more capable, or efficient, regardless of ethnicity.

The wrong thing to do is buy the "If you can't beat them join them philosophy! If that continues the majority of American Citizens will eventually score low on I.Q. tests, while the informed and aware will get smarter, more powerful and richer, and we will no longer have a race problem. The comparison will be like having troglodytes, of many races, against those who had vision, planned ahead, and met the challenge of living life, rather than kissing up to "feel good" solutions! The future of your children is decided by the quality of your decisions.

I watched in-laws and associates play the feel good game, and as their children grew I saw girls get pregnant to get welfare and boys go to jail, because they were taught that being cute and slick is more important than being skilled. My ex bragged when her nephews were buying nice things for her sister, knowing that they didn't have jobs. When they ended up in jail, the story changed to: "They are just like their father" whom they had not seen since they were very small. From those observations, I can imagine what will happen in that family over a period of just one generation. The original gene is from Africa, so Blacks will survive the nonsense, but at what cost, and at what economic, intellectual and spiritual loss?

As a youth I drew plans for the U-shaped ranch style home that I wanted and knew that it would be built on a hillside surrounded by a white fence. I wanted four horses that would be shared by my wife and children and was interested in Law Enforcement, but I would work hard and do a good job at whatever profession I entered. I listened to clichés that were designed to get us to live down to White expectations, and became aware of the socialization and training that causes us to fear taking necessary steps to become successful.

On my last trip to Mexico I visited the Mayan Ruins at Chichen Itza and was impressed with the information that was offered by this group of "Unconquered Native Americans". Caucasians spent time questioning what was said, because it contradicted the information that has allowed Europeans to feel superior. I went to segregated schools, was taught ideas that were contrary to what Whites wanted me to learn, and always felt that integration benefitted Whites who feared that we were gaining knowledge of self, which would allowed us to challenge concepts that are designed to hinder our social, economic and spiritual growth.

It was in the U.S.Air Force that I first saw blatant discrimination. I played base level basketball at Alconbury, in England, and in 1960 all but one of the Black team members was on the second team. At times when three or more Blacks were playing together and it looked as if we might win, we were benched and the team would lose, rather than expose that we might be better athletes than our Caucasian Teammates, so we barely won 50 percent of our games. I played in a tournament in London and was only allowed to play ten minutes during which I scored eighteen points and pulled ten rebounds. Our regular coach was not at the game, but told the interim coach, by phone, that I was to play only two minutes the following night. As a Black, Teammate was our best guard and, as the saying goes, "Could thread a needle with a pass" I hit ten points in two minutes. During our next practice session I was a "hot dog", "shot gun", "ball hog" and every other demeaning name the coach could think up. I came close opening a can of "Whip Ass on him", but I was also on the boxing team and refused to fight a battle, that would lose a war against a racist, incompetent coach.

The following year the base commander brought in a new coach who allowed us to play together, regardless of ethnicity. Coach Addison was a Texas A&M Graduate and his education served him well. He challenged me when I was wrong, but encouraged me when I was right. I remember thinking that I was better than other players, but was an alternate for the UK Tournament, so I approached him and expressed my feelings. He gave me a serious look and said "You are right and you will be suiting up". He then explained that he wanted me to view him as Jim Addison and not just some White Coach that wanted to tarnish the skills of Black Athletes. In 1963 the only team that we didn't beat was "Chicksands". When Chicksands won USAREUR their coach stated that the best team they played against, all year was "The Alconbury Spartans"!

Captain Jim Addison, from Texas A&M and Lieutenant "Huck" Smith, from South Dakota State were great athletes and examples that "Competent White Males" are not afraid of the skills of "Capable African Americans". In most life situations I have competed against Whites who have been promoted, based on friendships, politics, or family ties. Many had minimal skills, the brain of the ostrich, and the spine of amoebae, but I distinguish the difference between Whites who are more like me, than unlike me, in all aspects of life except skin tone. The ultimate loser in the game of "Ethnic Shuffle" is The United States of America.

Coach Addison was fair in practice and in games, so we won nineteen games before we lost, during his first season. He showed no signs of being openly unfair, but I was suspicious, because of the previous coach and angry, because promotions were being given to Whites who had not passed qualifying promotional examinations. Blacks had passed the tests, but were overlooked at the squadron level, while Wing Headquarters eventually demoted those who were not qualified. Being qualified, intelligent and neat in appearance was treated as insulting by some White NCO's. I was criticized for ironing and starching my uniforms, for the excellent shine on my boots, for getting scores above ninety five percent on all tests, and basically, for being a good soldier. I left Europe with 38 months time in grade for E-3.

My last experience in military sports was 1963 at Travis Air Force Base in California. The coach was much like my first coach at Alconbury, and like most of the coaches that I encountered in the years that followed. In California Black Coaches and referees proved to be more against other Blacks than many White Coaches and referees. I left organized basketball with a deep respect for Jim Addison, who was fair, insightful, sensitive, a winner and one of the few coaches that I ever considered a leader. He sent me to the showers when I did things that would negatively impact the team. He had a team to manage, but understood my Anger, and why I played tough defense on White Teammates I was damn tired of Whites getting special treatment (Affirmative Action), and he explained that it was to the benefit of the team that I played hard, but that my anger was hurtful to me and the team.

I was given E-5 when I joined the California National Guard, but was now a college graduate, with interest in a commission. I served in a military police unit, had military, campus and local police experience, and California Community College Instructors Certification to teach Police Science. I was told, by my commanding office, who happened to be Black, that my G.T. score of 135 was too high and that my records would be conveniently lost. He explained that such was common practice and that his experiences had exposed that it was better to be closer to the 110 minimum than my score. "My records were lost"!

In the Army Reserves, Whites were given temporary warrant officer status, when I, again, scored too high on the GT Exam. I was now in Colorado, and teaching a primary leadership course to an Engineer Battalion for the U.S. Army Reserve School. Frontier Airlines Managers refused to let me attend training, even as federal law required that I be given time off, so I was forced to resigned, and got no support from the military, or state government.

Unethical managers are smart enough to know when a spouse is an advantage for them against ethical, skilled, gutsy employees. Lee Iacoca talked about the poor treatment that good employees were getting, when he took over a Chrysler. My current employer is large, has a powerful legal department, and knew that they could outlast me, when I filed a discrimination suit. My attorney advised that it would take tens of thousands of dollars to win, what he saw as a legitimate case, and suggested that the challenge was close to impossible, because I didn't have the support of my wife.

Whites don't need to do all of the discriminating, when minorities aid and abet the cause by making decisions that are hurtful. Some Whites intentionally hire minorities who go along to get along, and the predicament is particularly debilitating West of the Mississippi. Dr. Naim Akbar has said: "If you want to escape the Armistad, the first thing you must do is slay the captor! I do not mean that you must kill anyone, but you must destroy the ideas and ideals that keep you in bondage"! The key to your bondage may sleep in your bed!

Chapter 26

While in the Air Force, I developed a plan and upon discharge I put that plan into action. I started my two pronged approach by applying for local law enforcement agencies and airlines that flew into and out of San Francisco. I, then, enrolled in college, where my experience proved to be much like my military experiences. Harold Banks, an African American Classmate and the most experienced officer on the squad, was passed over for the position of Chief of Campus Police and given a token position of Captain with no authority to carry out his duties, so when he made decisions and fellow officers refused to comply the chief usually decided against him. If a Black was insubordinate, the chief used such actions to eliminate any presumed possibility that his position was worthwhile. The individual who was appointed chief, later committed suicide after transferring to The University of California at Berkeley.

Harold tested for the San Francisco Police Department, scored 800 of a possible 1000 and was turned away, while a White Classmate was hired with a score of 640. He was eventually employed by the Palo Alto

Department, but his dream was to be a San Francisco Police Officer. In recent years I have talked with Harold, who was surprised that I remember the campus police incident, and explained that he fled a discrimination suit against Palo Alto and later Veterans Administration before retiring to a life of golf in Sacramento, California. Like Harold, I never used the "House Negro Modus Operandi" (HNMO), so after passing the California Highway Patrol Exam I never got a response. I took the Redwood City Exam and "supposedly" failed, but took the same exam for the L.A.P.D. and scored in the top ten percent among over three thousand applicants. Fairfield advertised in local papers, but always claimed that they had no openings when I attempted to apply. Daly City made claims similar to Fairfield, and San Jose's medical evaluator said that I had a back problem, but conveniently lost my x rays, when I asked to have them evaluated by a private doctor.

I was hired by San Francisco and spent my first year and a half, working Park Station in Haight Ashbury. I wrote a paper for an English teacher who suggested that I take one day off from a busy schedule and put some of my ideas in print. She sent it to The "San Francisco Chronicle" and my hometown newspaper the "Roanoke Times and World News" and both newspapers published it, so I immediately, got a lot of notoriety, and was quickly advised that the S.F.P.D. did not like Blacks who were too smart. I was the first Black Officer on the scene at the 1966 Hunters Point Riot, where White Officers were issued riot gear and shotguns, and I was not, so I stood out like a bean in a bag of rice! Maybe the department thought that I was dangerous, but Officer Burns, who worked with me at Park Station, handed me some of his "personal" forty one caliber ammunition. When I saw the concerned look on his face, I realized that my challenge was not from all White Officers". I saw that look often enough to realize that most police officers, regardless of ethnicity, were concerned about doing a good job under very trying circumstances.

Angry community residents yelled "Let's run these pigs out of our community and started throwing debris, until a lone voice from the crowd yelled: "Don't hit the Brother"! Which was followed by a chorus: "Yeah, don't hit the brother"! Later, the department marched the remainder of the Black Patrolmen onto the scene amid applause from rioter. Young Black Residents of Hunters Point were not unlike Young White Residents of the Haight Ashbury. Both groups were angry at a system that perpetuated dishonesty and abuse, but neither realized that parents had accepted the system and had therefore become an integral link in the chain of disrespect.

It was at this juncture, in my life, that I noticed that race is an issue, but there is a much larger issue that is camouflaged as is sex, age, and all the cliché's that small minds tend to zero in on. As long as we concentrate on nonsense syllables and cliché's, those who understand how the game is played will continue to grow, prosper and achieve power. Years later Congressman Parren Mitchell's Assistants explained: "The nation is divided into three groups, the average citizen, the outlaws and the bandits. The outlaws use threats, drugs, guns and terror to bleed off the average citizen, while the Bandits use the media, politics, coersion, threats, drugs, guns, terror, and every any other means to bleed off the average citizen and outlaws". Our governmental system moved from the military industrial complex to the information age, while the poor and unempowered moved to the age of welfare and prisons. In law enforcement as in politics, and business, the dirt often rises to the top, so my challenge is with those who are in a decision making capacity.

I decided that it is more important that I am happy and that material and power are not going to change who I am. The true test of quality of life is whether you are associated with good people who take you to a spiritual plane where nonsense is a non issue. To quote Reverend Jeremiah of Cleveland, Ohio: "Everybody that's your color, ain't your kind, and everybody that ain't your color, ain't your enemy"! I chose my associates based on what I think of myself, and I like me!

Months later, when I was transferred from Park to Potrero Station, I became known for respecting the rights of community residents, so leaders of Bayview-Hunters Point requested that I be assigned as the

Community Relations Officer representing their neighborhood. I tried to live up to their expectations and developed projects to benefit youths. Reporters came from Florida and Minnesota trying to understand why I could work in Hunters Point, which was then considered the city's most volatile community, and not carry a gun. I saw residents as like myself. I spent my early years in an orphanage, housing projects and a Segregated all Black Environment, so why should I be afraid? I went to All Black Schools until college and the Air Force wasn't really that integrated! The San Francisco Police Department was better than most, but still had a long way to go, in understanding ethnic and social issues. "Hunters Point was the norm for me in 1960's U. S. of A"!

Because of my new found notoriety, I was able to raise funds for community projects and "Was going to make a difference", so I got involved in more activities than I had time for. I was on the Board of Directors for The Law and Justice Task force, Local Development Company, Southeast Education Development, Bayview Hunters Point College, California's Coordinating Council on Higher Education and the Chancellor's Office for California's Community Colleges. I worked with the Education Consortium, California Youth Authority, San Quentin Squires, San Francisco State's Child Study Center, submitted proposals for funding, and had social, political and business contact with most of the city's leaders.

I was surprised at the attitude of some Black Officers who moved into the suburbs and acted as if they somehow changed skin tones. Some were most concerned about their pay checks, but there were officers, like Bob Jones, Bob Jeffrey, Don Daniels and Billy Wheeler who never forgot that we owed allegiance to all Residents of San Francisco, and that our job was to "Serve and Protect"!

I was a college student when Bob Jeffrey testified for a group of Blacks, because he saw a White Officer plant drugs on one of them. Billy, Don and Bob Jeffrey never let officers violate the rights of anyone and Bob Jones was so professional and perceptive that I felt lucky that I worked with he and Don on alternate days. I was coached, so I wouldn't overreact and can still recall Don telling me "You sit in the car until you cool down"! Sergeant Koenig and Sergeant Ryan were examples of White Supervisors who believed in excellence on the job, and like Don and Bob made sure that I did not expose my inexperience in critical situations. Caucasian Officers Ray Krutt, Wynn, Bertucci, Lieutenant MacFarland, Bob Ryan and many of my college classmates proved to me, that race should not be a priority and took my socialization to a higher plane. Hunters Point Residents liked Ray as much as they did Bob Jeffrey, but department managers failed to understand, "Because Ray was White". I had to work hard to compete with what Both had done for the community and still feel that Ray should have chosen, over me, as the Police Community Relations Representative. I was tutored by "San Francisco's Finest" and their teaching has benefitted me in every effort that I have become involved in since those years!

One day while working with an Assistant Principal at Woodrow Wilson High School, she made the statement that one of her Black Students seemingly had extraordinary potential, but needed some prodding to get him to do things. I asked of her, "What would you do if he was White" and she responded, "I would probably chew his butt out"! I suggested, "Why don't you overlook the fact that he is Black and try it"! A few days later she thanked me and mentioned that he had made a dramatic change. It was only after working with Ray that I finally got the message that "It isn't about race, it is about leaders taking responsibility and doing what is necessary to get the job done"!

In a police community relations meeting at the Alice-Griffith Housing Projects Officers Wynn and Bertucci stood strong and challenged a hostile, predominantly Black Audience to judge individual officers rather than incriminate the entire department. They challenged angry youths to admit that they, personally, had never treated any of the group unfairly. The teens agreed and focus turned to an individual officer who made a habit of finding painful ways to apply handcuffs, and whom youths felt abused his authority. He wanted to be like Chicago's Fabled "Two Gun

Pete" who, as legend goes, carried two pearl handled pistols and used fear as his primary weapon.

Officers Wynn and Bertucci then took on the parents who had no ideas about how to parent and often lied on children who had done nothing wrong, while failing to recognize the mischief of their own. These officers recognized that much of the anger originated in homes, but it was easier to fight against the department, and challenged youth to tell parents what part they played in making their lives miserable. It was at this meeting that I realized that youngsters were lashing out at all authority rather than direct it at a particular target, so teens challenged the most visible target: "The Police"! Dysfunctional parenting and a programmed environment of discrimination were causing problems that culminated in violent behavior. Meanwhile, parents with "Misplaced Values" left their offspring with no game plan, no direction, no sense of purpose and no hope; but children were unlikely to blame Mom, or Dad for this cycle of denial. With the precision of a surgeon, two kind, wise, experienced officers opened wounds and started some healing.

There were officers who abused their authority, but most were kind, descent and functional. One individual from my academy class who referred to citizens as punk, ass holes and sissies, was killed and the department tried to sanctify his image. Another did many things to infuriate Hunters Point Residents, and on one occasion had a violent argument with, Julia Comer, one of Hunters Point's "Big Five", Female Leaders about his wearing a "Gas Huey" (Newton) button on his uniform hat, while patrolling the Hunters Point Housing Projects. He was later involved in the, off cuty, killing of a Black Male and the department, "As Usual", found the shooting justifiable. The lawyer for the Police Officers Association was quoted as having called Black Citizens, who saw the incident, monkeys and hyena's. This so infuriated some Black Officers that we developed the "Officers for Justice" and did our own investigation, finding that, the department overlooked the testimony of key witnesses.

A month earlier the incident about the wearing of the "Gas Huey" button reached Mayor Alioto's office and one of the assistant mayor's, after a thorough interview, warned that this officer was going to kill someone. Assistant Mayor, Joe Brown, clearly stated: "His blond hair, blue eyed attitude is detrimental to good police work, and is a clear and present danger to ethnic minorities who reside in the City and County of San Francisco". The officer was later fired!

I was lucky to have lieutenant McFarland, at Potrero Station, so I did not have to go to managers outside the station when an officer and his partner stopped two twelve years olds and asked "Why don't you Niggers put your heads together and make a rock pile"! Bob Jeffrey, respected the Lieutenant and suggested that I go to him when I had a problem, so I did just that. At Park Station our lieutenant was referred to as "Cement Head", but I could always depend on Sergeant Koenig, Sergeant Ryan, Don Daniels and Bob Jones for good advice. At Potrero Station there were Ray Krutt, Wynn, Bertucci, Lieutenant McFarland and Bob Jeffrey.

After the 1966 Hunter Point Riot and my experiences in the Haight Ashbury I began to get a feel for how to do my job such that I would benefit the department and my community. I realized that I am not a go along to get along type and that I wanted to make a difference. I was unimpressed by parenting skills of community residents, or management skills of department leaders and felt that both did things that would prove to be wrong for the future of the city. There was an instance when I tried to talk a sergeant from the community relations unit into moving uniformed officers from Third and Oakdale, because I knew that residents wanted an altercation with the police. The sergeant turned to me and asked: "Why do we have to kiss their asses"? The situation worsened and a large crowd started to gather, until I called the Lieutenant in charge and requested that all uniformed officers be moved from the scene, allowing me an opportunity to dissuade rioters. He advised me that he would move the officers a safe distance, out of sight, but that I would be responsible, if things got out of hand. I agreed, because I knew that without blue uniforms and riot gear the situation would lose impetus. As officers started to leave the crowd responded with a massive "Aww, why are you pigs leaving"? Within minutes the disturbance was neutralized.

Chapter 27

I would be remiss, if I did not mention some of the community residents who aided my growth. Many who fell through the cracks during that era were young, intelligent Black Males who were committed, hard working and available, but there was no place in the system for them. The Bayview Hunters Point Community was strengthened by a group of ladies known as the "Big Five"! Elouise Westbrook was the best known of the group which included Osceola Washington–Means, Essie Webb, Ruth Williams and Julia Comer. Lillian Harrison, Beatrice Dunbar and others fought long and hard as a force against urban renewal programs that moved families without consideration for the hardship placed on those who were displaced. Mrs. Harrison was from Virginia and was the first person to tell me that I had to get over the notion that all Blacks were good people. She and Adam Rogers would say that I was naive to the things that went on around me, because I was too trusting of Blacks, simply because they were Black!

It was usually the males of the community who lost in the struggle, and of the early casualties was Mrs. Washington-Means son, but many of his associate also had run ins with a systems that showed no mercy. Of the more successful remnants was Gene "Bro" Mabry who went on to San Francisco State and worked on his Doctorate Degree, but left behind were the likes of Adam Rogers who was the first murder in 1976, and Jerry Collins who was found dead on Freeway "101". Adam's brother "Arthur", Robert and James Richards, The Bells, Mabry's, and Bishops, of which there many; Dupree Oklahoma and professionals like Harold Brooks could have been great had they been born with less melanin.

Reverend Lee, a Methodist Minister, was one of the realists who knew better than to get caught up in the nonsense, so he became a good "How To" source. One of my college buddies, who became a state policeman, pointed out a minister who was dealing drugs on my beat in the Haight Ashbury. The minister and his twin brother had taken over the church in Hunters Point that Reverend Lee had vacated, so I called reverend Lee and he, quickly, got them removed from the pulpit.

Arnold Baker, a lawyer and reserve military officer worked his way into the redevelopment agency hierarchy, Wesley Slade, was Assistant Mayor to Alioto along with Joe Brown, Doctor Washington Garner was Police Commissioner, The Reverend Cecil Williams, of Glide Memorial Church, L.P. Lewis and Harold Brooks also with the redevelopment agency, Willie Brown, the current mayor of San Francisco, Willie's Law Partner John Dearman, Gil White and Jim "Papa" Woods two staunch Southern California Republicans were like mentors as was Reverend Lee. Without some very good people who took time to recognize what I was trying to do and suggested a direction, I might have been lost as many Young Black Males were lost in the late sixties and early seventies. The reality of spoil system politics saw Whites pass a small percentage of the illegal funds, that they collected, to Blacks who went along to get along to get a share of the proverbial pie. Federal Agents knew that Whites ran the programs, but it was the Blacks who lost their lives were defamed, and too often, lost their will to continue the struggle.

I was impressed with Caucasians Leaders like Mortimer Fleischaker, Congressmen, John and Phil Burton, and Attorney Elkus, of the Law Firm Elkus, Bacigalupi, Salinger and Rosenberg, since each was always available for a just cause. All assisted me, or provided advise as long as I did the right things. Mr. Fleischaker always asked that I give his regards to Mrs. Westbrook and I liked going to Mr. Elkus Offices just to view his Native American Artifacts. The Burtons were there in crisis, or when I needed political advise.

I am fortunate that my parents taught standards, because I received offers and turned them down, but I am just as fortunate that enlightened leaders were there to guide me. Many who received funds from numerous programs, were indicted, imprisoned or killed, while I always proclaimed that my salary from the police department and later the college were enough for me and Estelle. "Estelle always had my back even when I wasn't sure of my next move"! I can remember talking with, then

Public Utilities Commissioner, Welton Flynn, who suggested that I seemed confused, when I had just finished a conversation with a young lady that I tried to inspire to enter college. His words were "Bill, you are in California and you must always remember that"!

When Adam was killed the rumors portrayed him as a sneak thief who had taken drugs from those who killed him. Rumors spread that he was tied to a chair and Clorox was poured into his mouth, and "Supposedly", he was hit on the head with a hammer each time he closed his mouth. Those who knew Adam never bought into the sneak thief idea, because Adam was 240 pounds of "Whip Ass" with a San Quentin Background. He was shot by the police during the 1966 riot and later shot in the back, neck and shoulder when he had a fallout with members of the Black Panther Party. Many say that he rode the city bus to San Francisco General Hospital from Gilman Street in the Bayview District with the three bullets in him. Most believe that he was killed to quiet him, because he had too much inside information. He was paid from federal program funds because of his brawn and killed because he could be not frightened.

I attended Black Panther Party Meetings when Adam and "Stokeley Carmichael" held meetings in The Hunters Point Redevelopment Agency Offices. On occasions when I was challenged by members who didn't know me, Adam, Arthur, Dupree, or one of a number of well known power brokers would suggest that I was a cop, but that I was okay. I got local party members involved in Police Community Relations Meetings which made police officials and some community leaders angry, but residents clamored to get in. Local politicians realized that this was an opportunity to participate in a community forum, so they also came. Like Bob Jeffrey, Ray Krutt and others, I did all that I could to try to find new ways to solve old problems, but the outcome was determined by opportunities that were available, from Caucasian Leadership, who agreed with us and wanted us to continue our efforts.

Chapter 28

On one occasion a group of us took eighty youths on a bus trip to Disneyland, but encountered problems when many of the adult chaperones failed to uphold their responsibilities. About a hundred miles away from San Francisco two of the group became very ill, so we stopped the bus, to find that someone had made drugs available. I used my authority as a police officer and suggested that I would turn away, but wanted all the drugs in containers that I provided. I was surprised at the amount of paraphernalia that was collected, but should have expected that one of the youths, a known prostitute, might use this as a business trip.

When we finally got to Disneyland one of the group decided to steal large items that he could not conceal, like sombreros, so we were in the park for approximately one and one half hours, before we were asked to leave. One of the buses had a broken door so we went to a motel to wait for the bus to be repaired. Some of the youths went into the swimming pool in full dress, got out of the pool, went into the rooms and sat on the beds and furniture, while soaking wet. I searched for the chaperones, but most were not to be found. When I questioned the youths about what they did many admitted that they had never seen a swimming pool before , so I asked whether they had ever crossed the Bay Bridge, or Golden Gate Bridge: "Most had not"!

When I got back to the city, I decided to start a program to have a swimming pool in the area and was assisted by a carnival owner who wanted to things for underprivileged children. We were able to get small parts for street club members in Steve Mc Queen's new movie "Bullitt" and we got other concerned business leaders to donate time and energy to see our efforts to completion. The carnival started out well, but almost turned into a riotous situation, because the number of those employed became so large that there was little money to share among workers. When the person who was designated to make decision about hiring, refused one of the neighborhood toughs he was punched and that started a chain reaction. I had advised the carnival whom not to give the decision making position, but he failed to heed my advise, so I had to work through my police contacts to thwart an inevitable altercation with the police.

Interestingly enough, when I moved to Denver I ran into one of the former street club members and asked, if he remembered me from San Francisco. His reply was: "Right, we were at City College together. I decided not to discuss where I really knew him from, because he was apparently doing well for himself. I met another former resident from San Francisco in Crystal City, Virginia, when I moved back to Baltimore, but it was apparent that he was still conning people, so he moved his office a few days after we talked.

I was as much like Ray Krutt as I was Bob Jeffrey and as time went on I found ways to do my job better, because I wanted to be a good police officer and not allow San Francisco's Racial Sociology to impede my efforts. As I grew into my career, I grew away from stereotypes and worked hard to become informed. Most Blacks are born Black, Baptist, or Methodist and Democrat, so it takes no genius to get you to this point.

When I make this statement to other Blacks, the standard response is, "I don't see how any Black could ever vote Republican"! I respond: "I had serious difficulty with Wallace, Faubus, Maddox, Helms and Southern Racist Democrats as a child, so I chose to broaden my perspective and vote for individuals whose records suggest that they are willing to respect me and my people". My effort has been to become informed, less dogmatic, more sensitive, caring and good at whatever I do and that includes understanding politics and economics.

Former college buddies, some who joined the police departments, some who became panthers; some who were Caucasian, and some who were Mexican encouraged me to continue doing as I was doing. I associated with a lot of really good people and steered clear of knuckle heads, so I felt comfortable that I could make the right decision in most circumstances. Some fellow officers approached me in the locker room and encouraged me to keep up the good work, while others, including Blacks, would "Publicly" start arguments to show that they were the good guys and weary of my tactics. Most admitted that they just wanted to do a good job and go home to their wives and families. I often wondered why I was sent to ethnic celebrations in cities outside San Francisco until one day I accidentally picked up a telephone and heard Chief Cahill tell Rodney Williams, Community Relations Unit Commander, to send me to a Cinco de Mayo Celebration in Richmond, because, to quote the Chief "He can talk to those people"!

In 1969 when I was sent eight small cards, in regular mail with a note stating: "Take your Hunters Point Buddies to the San Diego Zoo. I inquired about the charges, but nothing was done for almost a year until I decided to press the issue to get the problem resolved. I was too busy to waste time on what I thought of as nonsense, but my cavalier attitude almost proved to be disastrous. I was young, impetuous, invulnerable, inspired, and committed because I knew that I had done nothing wrong. The issue was not about right and wrong and, maybe, I should have done things differently. I forced the department into doing something that administrators may not have wanted to do. They were only trying to slow me down, but I was on a roll. I was charged with "Unofficer like conduct" because the department felt that I should have given my supervising sergeant an opportunity to respond to the tickets and the attached letter. Discipline was important in the 60's and I might have been charged with "Un officer like conduct" for missing a uniform button.

I didn't trust the opinions of a lot of people in those days, but later realized that the department's charges were proper, while media reporting was wrong. I credit California Assemblyman/Attorney Willie Brown; His Partner, John Dearman; Public Utilities Commissioner, Welton Flynn; Reverend Cecil Williams of Glide Memorial Church; Police Commissioner Dr. Washington Garner; Attorney Ed Dawley; Norman Jackson, owner and Chief of Cal State Patrol Service Wesley Johnson Jr., a local pharmacist; Preston Sample and some damn good policeman. with nurturing an upstart who wanted to do the right thing, but didn't have a clue about how, or why I was doing what I was doing. Like many of my associates, I was tired of injustice and angry at an insensitive system, but unaware of consequences and too involved to give a damn.

Attorney "Ed Dawley" represented me, but it was Willie Brown who advised that I was involved in an administrative proceeding and that was different from a legal action. He explained that while I had done nothing illegal, I needed to understand that those who manage the "SYSTEM" will defend against all challenges. He continued, "That I should not become cynical, but continue to fight with the understanding that I am an integral part of the system"! Dr. Garner met me at his office and let me know that he had to vote against me, but that he was still in my corner. Rev. Cecil Williams met several members of the community relations unit to show his support, while Norman Jackson, and Wesley Johnson Jr. encouraged me by telling me that I was a good person and that I was doing the right things. It was Norman who first to advised me that people were saying that I was too honest, and who explained why some don't trust people who are too honest.

After the many challenges to what I saw as an unfair system, I found myself unemployable, but I survived, maintained my standards and continue to challenge flaws in the systems armor, when I think that specific unethical actions will impede my children's progress. When San Francisco Police Officers claimed that they were lowering standards to hire minorities, research illustrated that the 82 Blacks, of 1800 total officers had median education of two years of college, while the median for Whites was eleventh grade. When my current employer was under consent for failing to hire qualified minorities I applied for positions and demanded that they prove that the person who was promoted instead of me had, at the very least, minimal qualifications. I demanded, under the letter of law, that my resume and the resume of the successful candidate be compared. The Human Resources Person who did the comparison finally transferred to another department, because she got tired of saying, "This, obviously, was not a practical decision"!

Once I graduate from San Francisco State, I found that I was overqualified for positions that were readily available prior to graduation. I took the G.R.E. and L.S.A.T. and went to Dallas with plans to continue my education. I wanted to go to SMU's Law School, but my finances and statements by the local D.A. challenged me to enter a master's program in Criminal Justice and Urban Affairs at the U of Texas at Arlington. I was rebuffed by Blacks in the class, when I suggested that the D. A. from Dallas' Presentation on how to keep minorities and females off juries was unconstitutional and unethical.

I, also, applied for the Dallas Police Department, but the investigator put false statements in my file, never thinking that I might be politically astute enough to get an opportunity to see the results of his investigation. My background investigation for the Justice Department was completed in Dallas by Justice Agent, Bob Greenwald who knew, then Chief of Police, Dyson.

When Whites and uninformed Blacks suggest that times have changed and we can't blame today's citizens for things that were done by ancestors,

I remind them of my segregated education in the 1940's and 50's, the discrimination in athletics and promotions in the Air Force in the 60's, similar discrimination in education and attempts to enter law enforcement in the 60's and 70's and my efforts to get fair treatment with my current employer in the 1990's. There is as much bias in our culture in the new millenium as there was during the time of our ancestors, and it is unfortunate that many are so insensitive as to not notice.

In 1973 I filed a claim against the Dallas P. D. and a White Federal Employee overlooked federal statutes until I went outside the region and had Bob Jeffrey, who was now a Regional Administrator in Seattle, advise Dallas that the ruling was in violation of Federal Statutes. It took fourteen years for me to get my first job in the airline industry, where I became an experienced, capable, hard working, exceptional employee. When I filed an EEO Charge against my current employer in 1995 a Caucasian Federal Employee overlooked federal statutes in the same way as was done in 1973. My 1995 claim was filed to make my company aware that there are still those of us who are willing to challenge an unjust system, while the 1973 claim was out of anger and the need to find a job.

Chapter 29

I found new friends when I moved to Colorado, but Lou Dodd, owner of Commercial Energies, Greg Scott, a State Supreme Court Justice and Thomas Jenkins, Director of O.I.C. and The Urban League, were strongest. I was given Lou's name by political contacts from San Francisco and Washington, D.C. and talked to him, by phone, for three years, before I met him in Chicago where we were organizing to stop Reagan Appointee "Cardenas" from destroying SBA's 8a Set Aside Program. Lou gave me access to Maryland Congressman Parren Mitchell, the nations strongest political advocate for empowerment through entrepreneurship, and Dr. Arthur Fletcher, author of the Philadelphia Plan, the last surviving member from Brown vs the Topeka Board of Education and known to many as the "Father of Affirmative Action". At this point, in my life I had grown beyond, "Party Line Politics" and was only into leaders who understood that leadership was about making decisions that benefitted all Americans equally, but with particular concern about the plight of Blacks, Hispanics and Native Americans.

Preston Sample sought me out, in Colorado, fifteen years later, asked me to go into business with him and was willing to invest $1.5 million dollars in a small business investment company wherein I was to manage the mid west region. A group of White Investors told us that their company would not do business with Blacks and when we complained that the statement was unethical, illegal and immoral, and that they were operating a bank that was certified by the federal government, the response was "Take us to court"! Even more interesting, the bank was started with a $500,000 promissory note and no cash, yet they were arrogant enough to turn down a program that would inject funds and a small business investment company which could use federal funds to grow to as much as $75 million dollars

In 1982, to my surprise, I was nominated by the county central committee, to run for Sheriff of Adams County. Lou Dodd advised me that I was in a win/win situation and that I should run. His explanation was that I was involved in many projects that were good for the community and that Blacks, Hispanics and others needed to see a strong minority candidate in the Republican Party. I garnered more votes than any African American had gotten in the state, in either party, in any prior election.

At a post election meeting, in Lou's Office, I was told, by a group of Blacks Leaders, that I was the first Republican that they had voted for and would probably be the last. They felt that I had shown that I was committed to uplifting the community, but that I was in the wrong party and the wrong city, because Blacks Residents of Colorado were not ready for new found freedoms. I responded that I had been both a Democrat and Republican in California and found little difference in the two parties. I explained that I was born without a choice of ethnicity, but with the ability to reason that some of the actions, "In both parties", were against me and my community.

One day while relaxing in the steam room at the Holiday Health Spa, in Westminster, I found myself engaged in conversation with a Black Male, a Coors Employee, that I had seen at the club, but never officially, met. He suggested that he knew me, but that I didn't know him and went on to suggest that I always tried to take people to a higher plane. He had seen my television presentation that won the "Colorado Starward" in 1982 and followed my campaign for County Sheriff. I told him that Whites complained that I frightened White People, but that the TV presentation was aimed at Blacks; advising what we need to do to better our predicament. We talked about some of the insensitive statements that we heard in the club, and particularly a conversation by a local minister who played racist jokes on youths in his church.

Apparently some White Children had parked their bikes in front of the church, which the minister moved inside. When the children came back to get their bikes, he told them that he saw "Black Kids" riding away on some bikes. Of course, the minister was upset when I suggested that with a three percent Black population in the county, I found it interesting that he chose Black Youths as the defining parable of his joke.

I was involved when D.J. Miller and Associates, from Atlanta, concluded that Blacks in Denver suffer a misplaced/displaced syndrome and I was involved when the Dahlia Mall studies were done in an attempt to improve the Park Hill Community. I was aware that a local newspaper study concluded that only 30 percent of Blacks realized that they were being discriminated against, while 70 percent of Whites admitted that discrimination was blatant. I was also aware that Lucius Ashby of the city's largest Black Accounting, current Mayor Wellington, and other political and business leaders utilized a concept of "Gate Keeping" to block the progress of qualified minorities, who did not go along to get along. I was not surprised when I read that Black Youths from Columbine High, stated in Newsweek Magazine: "Mom, Dad, we told you this was happening"!

I was involved with the Urban League when an employee of Coors told the story about jobs being advertised in November that had been filled in August, and know that this same employee left Coors and was unable to find employment, at his skill level, for many years. I submitted hundreds of applications in Colorado and got no responses, but came to Baltimore and was offered seven of the eight jobs that I applied for. I had eight years with Frontier Airlines and had applied for all airlines that operate in Denver, over and again for four years, but was hired at America west, in Baltimore, two weeks after I applied. One month after leaving America West I was employed by Northwest!

I talked to other Blacks who left the area and each explained that it was too difficult to find either business, or employment opportunities, while those who remain make statements such as: "I know people who are making lots of money here"! When I suggest that U.S. Department of Commerce Statistics show that Maryland leads the nation in minority business development and income, the follow up argument is, "There are more Blacks there. More is not the issue, it's about leadership, agenda, the level of awareness and the quality of the leadership in the "Black Community"!

I had no idea of my personal impact on a community until December of 1993 when I walked into "Bishops Store", on Revere Street in the old neighborhood in San Francisco and found that I was still being talked about, and I left San Francisco in 1972. I heard Bishop say: "This is the guy I have been telling you guys about for all these years"! People that I had not seen in twenty years were telling positive stories, to their young and my daughter was here with me, hearing things about me "That were good"! Now, here was a guy from my Colorado Experience who had a similar opinion! I now know that I can make a difference and that it has been worth the effort. I'm not rich, but I have left a trail of good behind me.

Chapter 30

My initial application, in the airline industry was in 1964, for a ramp service position with TWA, in San Francisco, and since I placed second on the test, ahead of the thirty three other applicants, I felt that I would be hired. I researched the industry and decided that I would learn and become a manager of a small station. From there I would prove my worth and begin a growth pattern that would benefit me, the Company and My family. In 1978, I landed my first position as a ramp agent with Frontier Airlines, in Denver.

My approach, again, was to learn as much as possible about airport operations, so I moved around until I felt I was ready to go forward and fulfill my goal. I was disappointed when I applied for a management position and Frontier chose an African American Male that other Blacks felt was the least qualified of all African Americans in the station. The company's choice was abrasive, narrow minded, arrogant and had difficulty communicating with other Black Employees. I had visited this scenario before, but hoped that things would be different with this company. I was aware that the only other Black manager that was close to us left a lot to be desired and was more of a smiling do nothing type, but I was still naive enough to believe that White Managers really wanted to promote quali- fied Blacks.

Frontier hired two Black Managers, at Denver Station, during my tenure and it quickly became obvious that they were hired to help termi- nate other Blacks, because White Managers were afraid of discrimination lawsuits. One complied and terminated Blacks when there was really no cause, so he was given a management position at Continental when we were taken over by Lorenzo and his scavengers. The other was terminated after a few months, because he was too simple minded to realize why he was hired.

In 1986, when Frontier Airlines was gobbled up by Frank Lorenzo's "Langoliers", I attempted to get hired by other carriers, at Stapleton Airport in Denver, and filed applications every six months for four years. I had friends at Northwest, America West, Continental and United, but my primary effort was NWA. My friend at America West suggested that there was a reservations center in Baltimore and that I might want to try the east coast. I was hired in Baltimore, but America West's Home Base is Phoenix, and after a few attempts I realized that they practiced "Safe Hiring", so there would be no promotion opportunities. When America west moved the reservations center to Kansas City I decided that I wanted no more of the insensitivity that I experienced in California, Texas and Colorado and would stay in Baltimore.

I started filing applications for employment with Northwest in August 1986 and my hire date was February 1992. I had eight years experience with Frontier Airlines, but got no response until I moved to Baltimore. Upon moving east I was hired in two weeks by America West and it took one month to get on with NWA, when America west moved their Reservations Center to Kansas City. I defy anyone at Northwest, or in any job that I have held to say that I am not one of the best and hardest work- ing employees.

After six years of applications I was hired at NWA Reservations in Baltimore with a group of two hundred forty reservationists from America West Airlines. Also in 1992, I found that the company was under consent decree, since 1989, to hire African Americans. Furthermore, I found that letters had been sent to African Americans Applicants, on the east coast, stating that they may have been discriminated against. "I never received a letter in Colorado, so I made attempts to contact the law firm (Springer and Lane) that was litigating the decree. I called and wrote many times, but never got a response.

Within a week the reservation manager was breaking union and company rules assigning seniority at Northwest Airlines based on hire dates at America West Airlines, rather than by last name per the union agreement. Others were allowed to change their last name on social security cards. For example Mike White-eagle became Mike Eagle and Carey Francis became Carey Butts. There was bantering to get the best seniority, so individuals falsified information about hire dates at America West, but when I contacted the human resources department and suggested that local management was encouraging unethical practices, I was told that the infractions benefitted minorities: "I replied that such a response was patronizing; that such actions violated CP and P and the union agreement, and that those who used false statements to get a job could, later, be terminated for falsifying job applications. I was not yet protected by the union, so I waited until I passed probation to continue the debate. I then found that employees had been allowed to change their last names back once to what they were before once seniority was established. Black Females who participated in these unethical practices suggested that I was a malcontent.

The general chairperson of the union, advised the local manager to follow union rules and those of us who had many years of industry experience tried to convince her that not following company and union precedence was encouraging distrust and creating an environment that is detrimental to the kind of esprit de corps that our new owners were working so hard to develop. Employees who lied, knew that there would be no follow up to check the information, but when I hear employees suggest that the company only cares about profits anyway, I suggest that I function as an employee in the same way as when I owned an ice cream store. This is about protecting my and my family's future. " The manager was later given another promotion"!

When a White Male Employee, wrote nasty, racist comments about Black Female Supervisors, we complained and produced a written copy of the statements, the company's response was to move him to Minneapolis and promote him. Two females, who were from Minneapolis, visited his new location, found what had taken place, and made the rest of us aware of this improper response to a very significant action. When I finally complained to the President and C.O.O., John Dasburg, he sent out a team of investigators and many of the shenanigans ceased.

I applied for the ramp from 1992 through 1995 and found that the station manager at B.W.I. was hiring off the street and bypassing the union agreement. Here was another Black Male using unfair, unethical tactics against Blacks to secure his position with the company. Once I got to the station, I found that he terminated Black Males only, which became a factor in his removal from the position.

Upon, finally, getting a ramp position, I transferred to DCA to get full time status. During my tenure there, a group of White Male Mechanics harassed an African American Male until Black ESE's came to his aid. There was no intent on violence, but as is usually the case, Whites saw the Black group as intimidating. When we met with management, it became apparent that we wanted the issue resolved and were not going to be sweet talked into taking a stance that would hurt us in the future. It also became apparent that the manager of the mechanics didn't have a clue, while again, qualified employees were overlooked. The Station Manager, Jim Hare, proved to be as unique as John Dasburg, in that, he did a fair investigation and took action to alleviate the problem.

I found the most favorable work environment, of my airline experience, as an ESE in Washington, D.C. where I worked with strong, principled,

Black Men who cared for their families, worked smart and acted based on standards that frighten go along to get along managers who are faint of heart. When I joined this group I was harshly challenged by those who thought that I might be a "sell out"! Later, I was advised that I met their standards and that I had a unique ability to communicate with young employees, while older workers only communicated among themselves. I was told that, originally, I was suspect, because I was too informed, too well educated and an ex police officer so it was believed that I was either a Black who frightened "The Man", because of my skill level, or just another "House Negro"!

I, probably, will not work with another group that is as strong, principled, socially and politically aware, and committed. I found a spiritual Mecca at DCA and wondered how long that scenario would be tolerated. Blacks in other stations referred to DCA as the only place where a "Brother can be a Brother", so I feel lucky to have experienced such an environment. It should be of some interest that DCA ranked as the best "A" station in the system, and was contrary to the stereotype that is so often portrayed of predicaments where the African-American Male may flourish.

When Jim passed away many of the Black Males transferred to other stations. Black Managers that followed learned little from the experience but employees will never forget. While this was one of the few situations where I have seen a group of Blacks, combine their strength for the benefit of one, I was even more impressed with the way Jim responded to employee concerns. Too often, we expect the few strong White Males that we encounter to work miracles, without realizing that they are struggling with the same exploitive system. There are minorities who cause this ethical few grief, because they don't trust, or because their "safe haven" is threatened, and there are those who just don't care to do a good days work.

For those of you who wonder how the Queen B Mentality impacts in this kind of predicament: "When I discussed the DCA incident with her, she suggested that the Black Mechanic should take a look at himself and try to choose a location where he would be more accepted, so the question that I put before her was: "Why is the victim at fault"? He is here to do a job and should be allowed to do that job to the benefit of himself and the company. I was not surprised by her response, because her lack of sensitivity is one reason why gets promoted company and epitomizes my example, of how companies support efforts that weaken the ties that bind good people together by supporting those with few skills and fewer concerns about others. It is easy to promote antagonism within groups by choosing those who bring less education, less commitment, less group ideals, less grit and more "I don't give a damn about anyone, but myself" into the mix.

I worked eighty hours a week and slept on the floor, in an apartment, for two years, to support her charge against her company", but when she won and got her settlement she became distant and arrogant. When she filed a false claim and took $68,000 from our insurance company, she came back to Baltimore to show me her check. She filed bankruptcies to cover excessive spending, so my business and political efforts had to be put on hold and when I needed her support she was a no snow.

Her credit habits hindered my borrowing to pay an attorney, when I filed an EEO Complaint, so I had to drop the case. She made it very clear that she did not want to get involved in my business efforts and got angry when I asked her to clean up her credit, not file another bankruptcy, or false insurance claim. I tried to get her to understand that smart employers do background and credit checks, so my efforts to get jobs, or become an entrepreneur is hampered: "She, obviously, didn't care"!

EEOC, like many agencies that get funds to resolve issues, is infiltrated by employees who get paid to overlook the law and perpetuate the problem. Non response is a byproduct of those who are hired, or promoted because they will not make waves, and while the approach is not always an attempt to exclude, the outcome is just that. When Whites experience exclusion, they jump on the "Reverse Discrimination" bandwagon, while overlooking the fact that White Managers make the selections under the guise of "Team Players"! These managers know that the selectee is often less competent, and that angry, un insightful Caucasian Employees, and spouses, will do what comes naturally!

When I filed a complaint with EEOC, a Caucasian Female Employee accepted the Northwest's claim that I had not applied for promotions and overlooked response letters, from the company. She was probably doing what she thought would protect her job, but once again: "At what cost to the agency that she works for"! There are many who are working hard to prove that EEOC is inefficient and want to disband the agency.

Meanwhile I was able to challenge the rejection letters through the human resources department, because we were under consent decree. Of those challenged, none of the selected had comparable skills, or experience, so the only response I could get from the lady who did the evaluations was: "The company made impractical decisions"! I guess she got tired of explaining and trying to make excuses, so she resigned from the department.

During one of my applications for promotions, I tried to get an African American Male V. P. of Air Cargo to assist me in applying for an air cargo position in Denver. I could have accepted that he chose a more qualified applicant, if he had responded, to at least one, of my numerous inquiries. If I had gotten a response, he could have told me that he had not received an application, which is unlikely, because a supervisor and one of the managers from B.W.I. Reservations talked to him, gave him a copy of my application, advised him that I had applied, and got his number, "from him" for me to call.

The company chose to overlook the seniority protest that I filed, in 1992, even as the General Chair of the Union advised the manager that she was in violation of the union agreement, and company policy. In 1998, during the pilots strike, I transferred to reservations, so I could continue working until the strike was over. I was paid $6 per hour less than my normal per hour salary, so I called payroll and made them aware of the discrepancy. To date, this has not been corrected, but in talking to a

Caucasian Female Employee I found that in that very same predicament the company immediately cut her a second check for the difference. My plight is not unlike that of many who came before me and many who will come after me, we face challenges in our homes and in the workplace. My lawyer, Attorney Nevitt Steele, suggested that we could win both the EEO and seniority cases against, but that it would cost tens of thousands of dollars and the company would outlast me. My effort was not to get money that I didn't deserve! It is about the future! "Your children, my children, your country, my country"!

In the 60's and 70's the buzz word was "multi culturalism", in the 80's "ethnic pluralism", and in the 90's "ethnic diversity". We didn't fix problems in previous decades, because power brokers are only serious about power. We simply add more "ism's" to the struggle, so the less insightful can decide which "ism" is most convenient for getting what "I" want!

When Robert Jeffrey became Regional Administrator with EEOC in Atlanta, in the 70's, he argued that Eleanor Holmes Norton's approach would give control of the agency to White Females. When I developed the course "Images of Women" for the Bayview Hunters Point College, Black Females from the community challenged the instructor to recognize the differences in the issues of White versus Black Females. They understood that Black were also being kept out of the job market, so women's liberation was not a benefit to Black Females at that point in time. The instructor made the mistake of bringing a Black Female Associate to preach her cause, but was rebuffed by female students who advised that the issues did not change, because a Black Instructor taught beside her.

In Denver, Public Service Company, gave a Black female a position on the board of directors when the company was charged with discrimination and since I knew her personally, I realized that like the associate in San Francisco, she would not raise issues that were important to the minority communities, and that is why she was chosen.

Uninformed Whites continue to blame affirmative action, while denying that preference agendas have always favored White Males and that

White Managers are making the bad decisions. Some of the blame must be placed on ethnic minorities, because it is necessary for an exclusionary system to have insensitive employees from ethnic groups, if it is to function as it does. Wellington Webb, Black Mayor of Denver, promotes a concept of gate keeping, which in reality, is nothing more than a way of blocking the progress of those Blacks who don't play ball as Whites have taught him that the game it is to be played. Two factors that were prevalent, when I lived in Denver: " The least capable, least threatening ethnic minorities got the jobs, and Insensitive ethnic minority female's were more likely to get hired and promoted, because they filled two EEO Slots".

The outcome is that we are divided within our homes. I read statements on the INTERNET that are written by Black Females who claim that Black Females are getting the jobs, because they are better educated, and that they are tired of Black Men blaming under employment on "The Man"! This is a strong argument for women who are "psychologically" stuck in the middle passage!

There is not much difference between my efforts in 1960's in the Air Force,1973 against the Dallas Police Department and 1995 against NWA. In each circumstance I entered the fray qualified, and ready to give one hundred ten percent, yet in each predicament less qualified applicants were hired, and promoted. I filed hundreds of applications in Colorado and got no response, but was offered seven of eight positions that I applied for in Maryland. Am I bitter? "No"! The challenge of living life to the fullest keeps me going, and I still remember the advise given to me by San Francisco Mayor, Willie Brown!

At Northwest Airlines I compete against Whites who have neither skills, experience, education, nor insight and proved that I was correct in my assumptions by causing a human resource specialist to compare the resume of the each successful candidate against my resume. True, A very capable White Male competed against some of the same applicants, was passed over and did nothing, but I remain convinced that, the selection of less competent ethnic minorities would have get cries of "Reverse Discrimination" that can be heard from the Atlantic to the Pacific Coasts.

Chapter 31

One of the advantages of living along the eastern seaboard is that White and minority employees talk about real issues. It is apparent, to most, that skills are not of primary concern when the decision to employ, or promote is at hand. I don't get angry at Whites who have no power to make changes, but I challenge ignorance and insensitivity and feel no empathy for those who are so into their tiny little worlds and can't see the big picture. Am I being militant, or realistic when I express Frederick Douglass' Philosophy, that "Until all men are free, no man is free"! Indentured servants and convicts were brought to the shores of the new world, and some Whites are as linked to the devastating concept of servitude and genocide as are Native Americans and other ethnic minorities.

I am also less concerned about employment, and business opportunities here, because there is empirical data that suggests that a small business venture may be the only real way to eliminate the kind of exclusion that is prevalent in our society. "The true road to freedom is not in seeking a job from those who dislike you, or hire only because federal statutes demand it. I am disappointed with those who have jobs, do them "Half Fast" and complain that they are being singled out, or harassed, and nothing irks me more than those who use laws that were designed to eliminate discrimination to cover their bad habits. I know my abilities and do whatever I do better than the next guy, because I am worth that to myself, my children, my community, and posterity.

Safe havens have never proved to be safe and going along to get along, has never been proven as a benefit for individuals, companies, or our country. Bad habits usually catch up with the worst of us and the world is changing so rapidly that many are losing positions that they were never qualified for. Those who have skated on thin ice, failed to develop real skills and abused others on the way up are not forgiven as they lose positions to down sizing and forced early retirement. Some, who were mistreated, are now in a position to decide whether those who rose on the backs of others, are worth considering.

The combined strength of Blacks along the east coast cause businesses to respond to discrimination complaints and to realize that they face a challenge. Many companies are comfortable with current practices, and socially sensitive ethnic minorities know that we have a long way to go toward eliminating unethical practices. Those who, initially, felt that diversity concepts might become an integral part of the corporate game plan now recognize that the "good old boy" system is now a "good old boy/good old White Girl" system, so few who have been promoted, are likely to support the advantages of seeking qualified minorities.

Many former activist suggest that the greatest counter revolutionary measure in the history of the United States was "integration", which weakened the solidarity of strong Black Communities and put Blacks and Whites who had little knowledge each of the other together. Now residents of a larger pseudo integrated community have even less knowledge of self.

When Blacks had to live together, we knew the sellouts, where they lived, how to steer clear of them and how to counteract their negative habits. Racism is no longer a cause, but an effect, so tax protesters, Minute Men, skin heads, the Aryan race, religious cults, the KKK and other White Groups now hate the very government that they once used to legislate exclusion. Meanwhile some Blacks, who don't have a clue about what is going on around them scatter into environments where they and their offspring are in jeopardy of physiological, or psychological denigration . Basic human rights are most often denied to people who lack insight, commitment, social awareness and political prowess.

Middle Class Whites believe that Blacks bring street violence to the suburbs, and Blacks who ran from cities to the suburbs "trying to escape reality" are finding that the only real change is topography. Drugs, drive by shootings, car jackings and malicious mischief are common today, so the peace and quiet that was once anticipated in suburbia is now fantasy. We had similar crimes in the roaring twenties when another drug "Alcohol" was illegal, but we did not learn from history. Meanwhile, social scientists and minorities term Whites fleeing from the inner cities as "White Flight", so "Black Flight" is a realistic term for Blacks who think that they can follow suit and escape reality by abandoning America's inner cities instead of analyzing the cause of problems and developing real solutions. Unsolved problems grow, fester and meet you at your door, when you are tired from that long, daily commute and have lost your sense of awareness just as you lost your sense of justice! You can't run, and hide and seek is a childhood game!

Some parents are unaware that it was they and their children who were the problems. They sell drugs in, or buy drugs from the inner city and continue to believe that relocating will protect them from issues that surround drug abuse. Urban centers have always been the center of activity for power brokers, because without people there is no power. To continue to move jobs from the city will erode all that has been good about America, and yes, it is unfortunate that mostly poor and minorities inhabit inner cities. The attitudes and habits of majority groups must

change, because by mid century there will be a change in the demographics of our nation: "The majority will then be in the minority"!

The war cry of "America is for American's" is mis stated, and "We don't
seem to care to know who the real Americans are"! "We still call them
Indians", because a "not too bright" sailor went the wrong way and "supposedly" discovered a land that was already occupied. Historians suggest
that Columbus landed somewhere in the Caribbean, and most still don't
understand that the borders of America stretch far beyond the borders of
the United States. The state of California is now home to over 10 million
Native Americans from Mexico and when we include immigrants from
Asian and remnants of forced labor from Africa it should become apparent
that the demographics of one of the most powerful sections of our country have undergone massive demographic change. A similar change is
sweeping through major population centers in the Northeast, South and
Southwest. Only the middle of the country is untapped, and that is going
to change.

In 1996 Continental Airlines was voted "Airline of the year", won the
JD Power award, had the highest increase of all companies in Fortune
Magazine's most admired ratings and beat us in on time performance, so
their stock doubled and split. Their success was reflected in filled seats,
while gatekeepers, in Minneapolis, maintained a bottleneck that damaged
us as competitors. Even as we made more money than the larger carriers
our stock prices remain low, because readers of business periodicals recognize that our middle management has not changed . Meanwhile there is
no real understanding that Northwest Airlines owns 14 percent of the
common stock and 51 percent of the voting stock.

Business magazines rank Southwest as the carrier with the best service
not realizing that "No Frills" means "No Service"! They compare meals,
advanced seat assignments, the ability to be transferred to other carriers,
have your bags transferred, and other "Frills to peanuts and a seat and
damage the efforts of major carriers. If there is a problem at any point en
route to your destination your only choice is Southwest and, if your bags

have to go to another carrier, you have to pick them up from the baggage and carry them to the next carrier. Editors need to take a closer look at staff and whom the magazines communicate with when doing surveys. Admittedly, being afraid to hire the best and the brightest of all ethnic groups has damaged efforts, but those whom we depend on to disseminate information must also be held accountable.

Dr. Arthur Fletcher stated in his "1970" report on the failure to properly utilize ethnic minorities: "By the year 2000, our national security will be affected by our inclination to exclude the best and brightest, because many just happen to be non white"! Our C.O.O. has develop the best scenario, since deregulation and employees can't see what he has done any more than investors, because periodicals disseminate misinformation. True competitors analyze shortcomings, develop strategies that overcome weaknesses and grow. I have competed against excellence and some who are not so good, but who excel by scheming and conniving. Usually the best get together and give each other due credit, while those who are less skilled work hard to hide their shortcomings, rather than work hard to improve.

I have found this to be true in most life situations and have confidence in my skills and my ability to perform, so I am not thwarted by those who fail to open doors of opportunity. I am concerned about the impact of those who would block progress, because I have children and my brothers and sisters have children that are taught that education, hard work and competence open doors. I have taught my daughter that a capitalist democracy provides many avenues to success, such that she does not have to compete against those who fear excellence. Real security occurs when one is socially and politically aware, competent to overcome barriers and driven to complete necessary tasks.

I am a competitor, have always been a competitor, will always be a competitor and many years of peaks and valleys have not cooled my desire to achieve my goal, so I never lost sight of the prize.

I have done television presentations, in California and Colorado, on the social and economic implications of poor political planning, and won the Colorado Starward in 1982, (local channel 4). for a television presentation on solving economic and social problems of minorities and the poor.

Taught classes at A.T&T. A.R.C.O. Coal Company, The Bayview Hunters Point College in San Francisco, Arapaho Community College and the Community College of Denver, O.I.C., Youth Services, The California National Guard, The U.S. Army Reserve School and for Evelyn Wood Reading Dynamics.

Written, planned, designed and implemented business, educational, athletic, cultural and social activities for community betterment, including funding proposals for profit and not for profit corporations, curriculum formats for college courses and an entrepreneur's academy for the city of Denver.

Been published in the San Francisco Examiner, The San Francisco Progress, the Roanoke (VA) Times and World News, Colorado Lifestyles Magazine and other publications and periodicals.

In 1982 I campaigned against an incumbent sheriff and garnered over 24,000 votes (43%) while spending only 7.5% of the amount of money spent by the incumbent. The county voting population was 3 percent Black and 85% Democrat: "I ran as a Black Republican". When I campaigned, for sheriff, the incumbent made the statement that I was not qualified to be his desk sergeant, overlooking the fact that I was better educated and had more law enforcement experience than he. I had a California Community College Instructors Certificate, experience with the San Francisco Police Department, the military police and campus police, compared to three years in the small town of Emporia, Kansas and no education beyond high school. I suggested that there are no monarchies, or blue bloodlines in this country and that he needed to stop thinking that an individual is qualified, because he, or she occupies a position. The incumbent, then made the statement that his greatest concern was that people might confuse our names and think that he was the "Black

Guy" because his name is Johnson and mine Delaney! He was sheriff because he was the "White Guy", but needed to be replaced, because he was incompetent, forcing himself on female employees and violating the tenants of his position.

Many was the time that I sat in Bally's Health Club and listened to White Males make excuses, for him, when he was charged with forcing female employees to have oral sex with him, or lose their jobs. One of the group was a minister who became incensed when I challenged his game of hiding children's bicycles and his church and telling them that he saw "Black Children" ride off with the bikes. Once the sheriff was deposed, the female who had the courage to deny his advances was put in charge of personnel.

I continue to challenge unethical practices, and those who know me respect my decisions. My years in law enforcement and my degree in psychology allow me a unique insight into misplaced values that are causing a decline in the quality of life in our nation. There is ample evidence that we must develop new approaches in dealing with the cancer of exclusion, if we are to survive and prosper. Many of us have worked hard and long to educate ourselves and we do those things that we have been told are right to become viable and responsible to our families and communities, but still find ourselves on the outside looking in! We have trained many with fewer skills for jobs that we were never offered and we have watched as doors of opportunity opened for those with less experience as we sat in the limbo hoping for opportunity to prove that we are worthy. Upon returning home our spouses have questioned what we did wrong, without understanding that it is what we did right that may have been our undoing.

To me the challenge of life is to continue to parlay my experiences to the children such that they will enter the skirmish better prepared than I was. Armed with information, intelligence and financing to fight the better fight, she will go forth and teach as my parents taught. I don't blame others for my errors and those of us who have, and will experience hurtful situations must learn to forgive, forget and prepare. The option is to become fearful, such that families fail, neighborhoods decay, and our cities becomes morally, ethically, spiritually and intellectually bankrupt.

My personal goal in 1990 was to build a small business, hire 100 inner city residents, develop an SBIC (Small Business Investment Company) and work with my daughter to help her, her brother and cousins to grow and prosper. I made the decision to move east based on information from the Department of Commerce, but Jacquie expressed distaste for my ideals and explained that she has no intention of ever living in an "All Black" environment. I find it hard to imagine living elsewhere and after divorce my finances have improved, so I enjoy my newfound freedom from her efforts to pull me to the dark side. My friends, my siblings and their families are my fountain of youth, but Baltimore is home and will remain home until I find a situation that affords me a better opportunity to grow and uplift others as I have been uplifted, since moving here.

When I chose to make this change, I developed an approach that is in tune with my college training. I knew that my next move had to be planned and in most cities Blacks prefer to be the big fish in a small pond, so they create blockage using uninformed peons as gatekeepers to maintain control. I prefer to be where a large group of successful Blacks are willing to create new ideas, rethink outdated agendas, keep lines of communication open and allow opportunity for a larger cadre of skilled infighters. I prefer to play the numbers! I know that twenty five out of a hundred Blacks in Washington, D.C. are making over $60,000 per year, while twenty of a hundred are making over $60,000 in Baltimore, so I moved to Baltimore. I mapped out the ten cities in which Blacks are doing best and found that seven of the ten are along the eastern seaboard. I later looked at areas where Blacks have the highest spending power and found the top ten to be in the south and east, with D.C. holding the number one position and Maryland being number two. In 1999 the State of Mississippi moved into the number two position, moving Maryland to a close third.

Family is more important, to me, than a big house, an expensive car and keeping up with the Jones', and I am not so naive as to believe that the majority of Black Residents in any city are in touch with reality, but the statistics are overwhelming. Maryland has a legacy of qualified Black Leadership from Frederick Douglass to Thurgood Marshall, Congressmen Parren Mitchell, Kweisi Nfume, and Mayor, Kurt Schmoke. Prior to the civil war there was an equal number of slaves and free Blacks in Maryland and five years before the "Emancipation Proclamation, a Black Man owned a business, on Baltimore's Wharf, that employed over 1,000 employees, both Black and White!

Reginald Lewis, a Baltimore Native, took Mc Call from $15 million dollar business to a $90 million dollar business, then purchased TLC Beatrice and became the richest Black man in America. Now We Have Cathy Hughes developing Radio One to a 1.3 billion dollar business that is befitting of Baltimore and in Washington, D.C. Robert Johnson recently merged B.E.T. into Viacom for 2.33 billion dollars in stock and the elimination of debt. He now plans to develop D.C. Airlines and is purchasing part of a hotel chain. "All this and no mention of the "Crab Theory" that is often discussed west of the Mississippi. "This must be the road to sanctuary"!

In seeking opportunity to develop a small business, in 1990, I found that Maryland led all states in the number of Black-owned businesses as a percentage of the total population. The top 10 were:

State	Black owned Businesses	Businesses per 1,000 population	Percent of total businesses
Maryland:	21,678	4.78	8.9%
South Carolina:	12,815	3.74	8.6
Mississippi:	9,667	3.68	8.6
Louisiana:	15,331	3.45	7.5
Georgia:	21,283	3.42	7
Virginia:	13,781	3.18	6.3
North Carolina:	19,487	3.04	5.9
Alabama:	10,085	2.47	5.7
Delaware:	1,339	2.16	4.5
Tennessee:	10,423	2.15	4.1

(source: Bureau of the Census 1989)

*1992 statistics were comparable with Maryland then having over 35,000 businesses

In reviewing income patterns I found that of Baltimore was number two when ranking the cities where African Americans have income at, or in excess of $60,000 annual. The top ten were:

Washington, D.C.	23.4%
Baltimore	19.1
Houston, TX	14.2
New York	11.7
Los Angeles	11.2
Chicago/Detroit	9.6
Atlanta	8.8
Philadelphia	7.9
Dallas	5.1

(Source: Bureau of the Census 1990)

STATES WITH THE HIGHEST PERCENTAGE OF TOTAL BLACK BUYING POWER, 1999

Washington, D.C.	39.1
Mississippi	20.8
Maryland	20.4
Louisiana	18.6
South Carolina	18.1
Georgia	17.9
Alabama	15.4
North Carolina	14.3
Virginia	12.8
Delaware	12.4

(Source: Selig Center for Economic Growth, The University of Georgia)

In analyzing housing costs relative to business and income potential I found that: "The median value of all owner occupied housing, in

Baltimore, in 1990 was $54,700 compared to a statewide median value of 116,500, well over twice the value of city housing. The average value of owner occupied single-family detached homes throughout Maryland is 164,414, but only 102,309 in Baltimore. The average value of owner-occupied single-family attached houses statewide is $88,243, but only $52,854 in Baltimore. While Baltimore contains 15 percent of the states total population, 56.6% of all owner-occupied housing in the state valued at less than $50,000 is in the city. Baltimore, the 19th largest metropolitan area in the country, has the 9th largest African American Population and is the 5th richest minority marketplace behind:

1) New York
2) Los Angeles
3) Chicago
4) Washington, D C.
5) Baltimore

Maryland had the most affluent and highly educated African American Population in the nation! Of all states with at least a 10 percent Black Population and a Black Population of more that 1 million, Maryland had the highest median "Black" income.

(Source: Bureau of the Census 1990)

Finally, in June 2001, Black Enterprise Magazine completed a survey of 4,239 internet surfers and combined their responses with socioeconomic and demographic statistics to chose the ten best cities for African Americans. Seven of the ten have Black Mayors, half of the ten are located on the east coast, and all have a Black population of at least 25%. Editors at Black Enterprise were wise enough to state where opinions did not jibe with facts. The top ten were:

	Percent Black	50k plus income	Mortgage rejection rate
Houston,	25.3	13.1	40.57
Washington, D.C.	60	28.4	24.77
Atlanta,	61.4	15.1	30.63
Charlotte, No. Carolina,	32.7	10.9	n/a
Memphis, Tenn	61.4	8.2	36.18
Detroit, Michigan,	81.6	16.3	36.21
Baltimore, Md.	64.3	17.0	28.89
Dallas	25.9	12.1	40.71
Chicago	36.8	18.2	32.68
Philadelphia, Pa.	43.2	16.1	28.64

You will notice that I chose eight of the ten in 1987, so the information did not change drastically over two decades. I moved my daughter from Denver to Baltimore in 1992.

In 1968, a Carnegie Study for The University of California at Berkeley cited: "Lack of academic achievement is a realistic adaptation to America for Blacks, Hispanics and Puerto Ricans, because once they get the education they still don't get the jobs." A follow-up criminal justice study by San Francisco, San Mateo and Alameda counties, in California, exposed that unemployment, family lifestyle and lack of academic achievement are the major factors affecting juvenile delinquency. The Kerner Commission Report (1968) verified these findings, and a report by Dr. Arthur Fletcher (1970), stressed that, "By the year 2000 America's national security and economic prowess could be threatened by our inability to utilize the intellectual potential of ethnic minorities, who by then will become the majority of the national labor force!"

During my college years in California in the 1960's and early 70's I noticed that Competent African American Males experienced a horrific downturn in economic opportunity during their mid 40's, and that the suicide rate for African American Males was three times that of White Males during that same life cycle. The prevailing myth in the community, was: "Blacks don't commit suicide" and There is considerable concern about the destruction of the African American Male between the ages of 18 to 25, while we overlook important statistics about those years that are most productive for the Caucasian Male, but are the opposite for African American Males.

In a USA Today article date 25 February 1993 Tony Brown, host of "Tony Brown's Journal" was asked, "What is the state of Black America?" His response was: "When the doors of integrated opportunity were pried open, the middle class beneficiaries of preference programs moved in with their socioeconomic non-Black peers. Now let us suppose that everyone in England who graduated from college and earned high wages moved to France? England would become a slum, while France prospered." That is precisely what happened in America's inner cities!

Arthur Okun identified a general economic trend, now known as Okun's law, by studying how unemployment changes with the growth, or stagnation of the nation's economy. He concluded that the economy had to grow, for a year, at a rate of two percentage points above it's long-run trend of 2.25% for unemployment to decline by one percentage point. In essence, it takes a growth rate of 12.5% per year to bring general unemployment down from 10% to 5%, so we need to face the reality that the federal reserve is unlikely to allow a growth rate that will give African Americans an acceptable level of employment. We comprise 20% of all unemployment, but make up only 11.2% of the nation's labor force, and this racial disparity has not changed significantly. As long as employment of African Americans is presumed to "trickle down" from general full employment policies, this racial disparity will remain.

In examining 722 of the most successful African American Firms in Atlanta's Metro Area, I found that 77% of their employees were Black, that the firms were, overwhelmingly, located in Black Communities and that 21% of these employees were from low-income, inner-city neighborhoods.

"The most effective way to curb unemployment, decrease inner-city violence, improve academic achievement, change family lifestyles and raise the self esteem of Blacks is to promote the growth of African American owned businesses. "

(Source: Thomas D.Boston, Professor of Economics at Ga. Inst. of Technology

We need to view ourselves as part of the global community and focus on what we need to prosper as a group. The challenges to the group will dictate the opportunities for the individual, but we are perceived as disorganized, disjointed, disgruntled, mis-educated, misled and missing in action on the economic battleground, while the rest of the global community realizes that power lies in ownership of communities, businesses and leadership. Theodore Cross, author of the book "The Black Power Imperative" suggests that we lost control of the civil rights movement when we stopped paying for it. He continues: "We started by having fish fries and other events to raise funds to support our activities", but later sold out to large corporations and big government. He uses the analogy of Detroit Edison giving a quarter of a million dollars to the Urban League to help us find jobs, while installing a two million dollar computer entry to assure that we weren't hired at Detroit Edison.

Most of us who were active and informed, during the sixties and early seventies, were aware of the actions of American Corporations that sold us a line of B.S., while blocking access to "Mail Rooms and Boardrooms. We were aware that Richard Nixon, "The Republican that America loves to hate", widened the door to economic opportunity with his "Black Capitalism Concepts" and that "Uncle Tom" was a warrior in the fight for equal justice, rather than a wimp who turned his back on the struggle. In attempting self empowerment we expected nothing without maximum effort and surmised that there was little difference between democrats and republicans, or liberals and conservatives in their valuation of the Black Experience. We asserted:"A liberal will give you the shirt of his back, but will keep one arm in one sleeve, so he can tell you how to wear the other", and we knew that many Blacks criticized the civil rights movement as did some members of the White Community. Blacks who sat on the fence and whined and complained that we were troublemakers, were later hired by those who were afraid of righteous challenges and but paid homage to the old "James Lynch" con of pitting Black Male against Black Female, youth against the elderly, light skin against dark, poor against the middle class,.......! Likewise, our motto became, "If you can't dazzle them with your brilliance, baffle them with bull shit"!

If you don't want to live among your peers, you don't have to, but your conversation should reflect lack of interest, rather than a negativity that suggests that you are somehow better. Clothes, cars and a big house do not mean that you have class, or that you are safe. If you are lucky enough to leave a bad situation, be thankful, but if you got there using immoral and unethical means, be very afraid! One of my Colorado Associates explained that he knows the reality of the Black Experience and that he could probably do more, but he just doesn't get involved, because that is his way. I never heard him make negative statements about the Black Community, or Black People, so why belittle him.

On the other hand, there are those who need to do some soul searching and raise their level of consciousness. To nonsense statements, such as I don't believe in statistics, I suggest: "I can recommend a good math course that will help but, if you are only interested in yourself, be honest and accept that as a fact". To the socially insensitive, I suggest literature that is written by Blacks, Hispanics, Jews,....", ! The option is that, to others, you sound like a closed minded, uneducated, bigot regardless of your ethnicity.

In Search of Sanctuary

Chapter 32

I can recall watching a trial on court TV about an ostrich burying it's head in the dirt under a fence, while on the other side of the fence was a rottweiler. Each did what was natural: the ostrich buried it's head, and the dog bit it off. Now here was the owner of the ostrich seeking damages in a court of law. I immediately thought about the four Black Females on the jury for the New York City Policemen who fired 41 bullets at unarmed Diallo, striking him 19 times. Prosecutors are good at finding the socially impaired.

Many Blacks don't have a clue about what is going on in the Black Community. Studies show that 79 percent of Whites and 42 percent of Blacks are ethnically insensitive to Black Issues. I believe that the larger percentage of that group are females and many of the remainder are the children of that same group of females. Our national media is replete with myths, and many of us get upset when our ignorance is challenged, thus we are quick to argue our rights without accepting the fact that we have a responsibility to ourselves, our children and our nation.

Imagine how those ladies will feel, if a relative should encounter the police unit that harassed forty five thousand Blacks and Hispanics to get nine thousand arrests of which only two thousand went to court. The Judge and prosecutors charged the officers with every possible crime, so they can not be tried again except under federal law for civil rights violations. Will they be charged as being responsible for the death of Diallo under civil law as O.J. was charged, and what do you think the outcome will be. Now we find that the Ramparts Division of the Los Angeles Police Department is guilty of similar atrocities. Surprise! Surprise!

I understand my fetishes, wants and desires in comparison to my needs, and that it is necessary to sacrifice, if I want to achieve goals, or obtain desired results. I was not surprised when my sister in law told me how shocked she was with my recent choice of a wife, because she knows that I am turned on by dark skin, round firms hips and a nice butt. I guess I had to grow up, because I feel that I have found my sanctuary with a retired professional from the Philippines. While just looking at some Black Females light my fire, my current wife puts effort into making sure that I am happy. She is supportive and doesn't use mis communication as an excuse. When some women say we don't communicate, they really mean: "Up his, I am going to do what I want, and I don't care what he, or anyone else says, does, or thinks"!

Edita was in the U.S. on a visitors visa, and employed by a Caucasian family that lives in Virginia, when I met her. The husband, of the family, was born in the U.S. and the wife in England. During her tenure with the family she was employed as a nanny who tutored the child, and kept the home clean. There was an obvious attempt to get her to marry a Caucasian male friend, which failed, so when the family was advised that we were to be married, the wife asked whether I was "Black, or White". When Edita answered "Black" the wife responded "That's horrible", to which she replied, "But I love him"! The next response was, "We no longer need your services"! Edita was upset, because less than a week before she had been told: "I don't know what I would do without you"! The previous nanny was from Cambodia. Was she was legal? Did she have a work visa?

I explain, to Edita, that such has been my ongoing experience as an African American reared in the U.S. I hope that such an incident will not change her natural tendency to be a sweet, kind and decent. I, then, suggested that I survived America's insanity by developing a personal concept of sanctuary where I can go and leave all of the craziness that makes one feel that he, or she is being misused. I call this place home, but for many, home has more nonsense and less security than the workplace, or the streets. Home should be a place where one can express love, feel loved and recuperate from the ills that we encounter when we pass through our doors. Home should be more than a shelter from the cold, or place where one eats and sleeps, since you can get that at a YMCA, homeless shelter, or hotel. In sanctuary all residents are partners and supporters and should remain so until one violates a code, standard, or rule that must be maintained for the benefit of the group.

All who reside in sanctuary must realize that there is to be no love, without nourishment, and no strength without effort to be strong. We must acquire information and develop an agenda, if we are to have ideals. Some will need to reconstitute themselves and realize that to do so will require an investment of time, energy and purpose. The difficulty of the task will depend on just how far one is removed from that reality which makes each an integral part of sanctuary.

My search was for a sweetheart and I found in Edita what I had been looking for. My daughter and I have had been spiritually teamed for many years that I felt it would always be that way, until she came along and added a partner to our efforts. When I ask females: "Are you a sweetheart"? The standard response is: "That is for you to decide"! "WRONG ANSWER"! When I asked Edita her response was, "OF COURSE"! It is an individual's decision as to the kind and caring, and we need to stop blaming ugliness on life's experiences.

Edita is well educated, as are her siblings, and they communicate a group, a family. My brother and sister in law recently gave us a van, because they purchased a new S.U.V. I thought back to the car that my ex wife sold to her friend and co worker's son and by comparison this van was a far more quality vehicle. I was surprised, because during our twenty five years of marriage, the only giving person in Jacquie's family was my father in law. During my years with Estelle, friends and family were as giving and caring as were my parents were, but there were few resources to share.

In talking to Edita I found that among her parents and siblings, all family resources are spent to give children an opportunity for an education. Edita's parent sold their land to educate ten children and her sister's husband sold his land to get twelve children through college. We discussed starting a business and she has told me that she wants to export and import goods between the United States and the Phillippines as soon as we can save enough money.

I decided, early in the game, that nobody was going to make me into someone that I did not like, and that I was going to work hard to assure that I was unique. When someone questions my character I stand strong and verify my qualities, just as Edita does. If I wanted to be a jerk, I would not deserve a sweetheart, so I always take the "HIGH ROAD", and taught my daughter to travel that same path. I was reared to believe that a good man has integrity and pride, and strive to be all that I can be: "Such is my destiny".

During the twenty plus years that I spent with Nicole's Mother my life was in a negative mode, so I worked hard and accomplished little. My years prior to her were good and in the year that I have been divorced it is as if I am again growing, prospering and doing worthwhile deeds. There are natural laws in the universe that allow us to develop in a particular direction based on decisions that we make. I feel as if I have been in a slingshot that has been inching backward for many years, but is now moving forward at a rapid pace.

With Edita I inherited good in laws, who share and care for each other. My ex, her family and friends always kept ugly secrets and life was about money and image, so no one trusted the other. On one visit to Texas An elder aunt, my ex and lady friends bragged about things that they did to men, but all were all afraid of Jacquie's father, the one family member that I still respect. He did all he could for his children, never looked for hand-outs, and gave when he felt there was a need.

Chapter 33

IN SEARCH OF SANCTUARY

If you were diligent, you noticed that my format has been to start with family, move into the work environment and, on to sanctuary, but at each juncture I seek solutions. Developing solutions is a habit that I acquired during my activist years, while participating in community projects. During the 60's when we met with business, social and political leaders, the first question was: "what can we do to help you"? It was apparent, to me, that business, political and social leaders knew what we wanted and needed, but when we came with no solutions, they were able to overlook us and do as they had always done. I found that I was usually thrown more crumbs, because I came with answers. I was also the one that the system worked hardest to discredit, because I put effort into staying current. Opinions should be based on information, and my training in social learning theory caused me to see ideas where others saw generalizations.

When my youngest brother's firstborn was married, I stayed, with my sister, a brother and his wife, my daughter and two nieces at the

Residence Inn in Minneapolis. Because of things that we have known others, including in laws to do, my daughter and I were, particularly, attracted to a framed message that was placed near the breakfast area. The message stated:

"A man wrote a letter to a small hotel in a mid west town he planned to visit on his vacation. He wrote:

> I would very much like to bring my dog with me. He is well-groomed and very well behaved. Would you be willing to permit me to keep him in my room with me at night?

An immediate reply came from the hotel owner, who, said:

> I've been operating this hotel for many years. In all that time, I've never had a dog steal towels, bed linens, silverware, or pictures of the walls.
>
> I've never had to evict a dog in the middle of the night for being drunk, or disorderly. And, I've never had a dog run out on a hotel bill.
>
> Yes, indeed, your dog is welcome at my hotel. And if your dog will vouch for you, you're welcome to stay here too!"

I thought about all the items that were taken from the many hotels that I stayed in with my ex, and the time a sister in law left a hotel in their home town, after a high school class reunion, without paying the bill. She never thought about the fact that her father was well known and still lived in that small town. I thought about the scams, the arguments, tacky associates and unethical relatives whose activities were an unwanted part of my life for so many years. Such problems are now gone from my life, and in their place are warm, friendly, considerate in laws and associates whom I am proud to spend time with.

I developed poems that reflect my feelings about my relationships with wives, in laws and family, and a an exam to help you get a clearer understanding of friends, associates, or a significant other. My family experiences, during childhood, were much like those portrayed in the movie "Soul Food", while many of my west coast experiences, are more like the movie "Friday!" My poems reflect the comparisons and the exam is an effort to recognize differences in individuals. My first wife was low maintenance and high profile, my second was high maintenance and low profile, and my new wife is low maintenance and high profile. "I came from a low profile, low maintenance background".

Star Jones of "The View" would be a likely example of high maintenance, because she obviously has expensive taste. However, she is high profile in that she has garnered personal skills to maintain her desires, rather than take advantage of someone else, her qualitative approach and her ability to make things happens for herself offsets the negatives of being high maintenance. A low profile, high maintenance example might be Robin Givens mother in her efforts to marry her daughter to Mike Tyson's money and popularity. Low profile females are all over the place; flaunting bad taste, bad manners, and no class, while telling us how good they look, and that they don't give a damn what we think.

The concepts of sanctuary, maintenance and profile were developed in conversation with a Black Male, Reservations Manager with Northwest Airlines. I was in a marriage that was doomed from the beginning, when we talked about the difficulty of finding good women, because so many females have bought into the dark side of the system. Craig understood, when I demanded a principle of fairness, and I knew that I had to follow rules such that I did not violate his position. He assisted when I tried to contact the company's Vice President of Air Cargo, about a promotion that would have gotten me back to Denver. He talked to the V.P., who happened to be Black, advised him that I had applied, and got his contact number, for me. The company, during my EEO Complaint, denied that I applied for the position.

We agreed that humans seek a supportive, understanding and caring environment in which we can coexist with families, friends and associates, but theorized that Black Males are less likely to find such an environment, and more often in jeopardy from negative influences. As Black professionals, we often, find it necessary to respond to one sided perspectives on relationships, blasphemy from the media, name calling from Whites, and innuendoes and put downs from some African American females. We agreed that the tables have turned and name calling is now aimed at women.

Because men talk to men and women talk to women, we often talk at each other when we finally get together and God forbid that when we "Talk At" the opposite sex, either person is interested in a sexual relationship. If you discuss your significant other, it should only be with those who are capable of maintaining secure, healthy, worthwhile, relationships and who don't see you as a mark, because nothing is more foolhardy than discussing important issues with one who cannot maintain brevity in his, or her own life. We all need the courage and insight to be honest.

One option is that you will end up in a relationship like the one with my second wife who finds good men and get them to believe her, while women give her "immoral" support. I thought she would learn when her sister went to jail, but she didn't! When she was arrested, she didn't learn and when her health went bad and she started losing her eyesight, she didn't learn! She once told me that Black Men aren't devious enough and that I am too honest. I have the love and respect of my children, good health, a good job and good friends, while she has money, the house, furniture, a lonely bed and a shaky future. Change is constant and some lucky people grow up!

I realigned some ideas from Ebony's "Sisterspeak" and "For brother's only" that might help you decide, if she's for real, or a keeper? She's a keeper if:

1. She knows that there are four quarters in a fiscal year.
2. She knows that there are four quarters in a dollar.
3. She is just as eager to climb a wooden ladder as she is a corporate ladder.
4. She doesn't think she knows it all, nor does she think that you know it all.

5. She doesn't think that somebody she compares you to knows it all.
6. She is hard enough to stand up to you and soft enough to cry in front of you.
7. She knows that neither of you is perfect, but always strives for perfection.
8. She laughs at your jokes and realizes that it was a joke.
9. She sets out to change the world, but doesn't set out to change you!

She's for real if:
1. She never lies to you, but casts the truth in a positive light.
2. She treats your children like they are diamonds in the rough.
3. Holds your hand in public.
4. Makes you feel like the alpha and omega in her life.
5. Pampers you whether you are sick, or in perfect health.
6. Supports you at home as much as she supports your efforts on your job.
7. Wears that special dress just because she knows that you like it.
8. Tells you her most guarded secrets and most sensual sexual fantasy.
9. Keeps you coming back for more!

One sign that she may not be emotionally mature is, If she uses profanity, as many "I KNOW I HAVE CLASS" sisters do, and if she expresses a belief that women are more mature than men: "You have a problem"! The maturity issue allows her to criticize everything you do and to believe that she is always right. There are women who like bad boys and, if they don't get over it by high school, many spend their lives shuffling through refuse bins for mates. If that's where you were found and neither of you understands that you must change, you are likely to remain dysfunctional, so "Please don't have Children"!

Males, on the other hand, need to realize that we must invest before we have a right to expect a return. A drink at a bar, or dinner at an expensive restaurant may not be a door opener and you shouldn't expect that you will get something every time you give. Uneducated, unsophisticated, unaware, misguided, young fools, who are in training to be old fools, should not want a sweetheart. If you want a good woman, remember one rule: "LIFE GETS BETTER AS YOU GET BETTER"! If one of you is trying and the other is not, the one who is failing to perform is causing drag, and no one needs a significant other who creates burden. Accept the fact that your mistakes are yours and and stop justifying your foolishness, while the rest of us are trying to live as responsible adults.

If you listen to women it is the men who are doing all the cheating, so again I refer to Ebony and reflect on the December 1998 Issue about why women cheat. It has always been apparent, to me, that the numbers implied, by females are insane. The implication is that large numbers of men are cheating with a very small number of women, so this group has to be super women. Most of the cheating men that I know have four and five women, so the numbers don't work, and math is an exact science. If a cheating woman has four to five men it would make sense, to me, that men are cheating at a rate of five to one. However, As I read the article I was particularly impressed with the paragraph titled "Sugar Daddy Search" and I am quoting a section of this paragraph verbatim, because I recognize the scenario!

"Due to her own character flaws, she is attracted to men with money, power and position. When she has an affair, it is more about getting the material goods that she feels are missing in her life. She remains in her marriage and may even love her husband, but gets the "whip cream" by engaging in an affair with a man who can provide her with furs, diamonds, travel and cash. She is primarily in the relationship for what she can get out of it. Dr. Berry says when she counsels women about the risks that they are taking, they often express no guilt".

We must question the integrity of men and women and stop placing all the blame on men. Queen B and Player mentality is great for entertainers, but in the real world neither has any redeeming social value. When we look at Jerry Springer shows, we want to say that its all a set up and off times that is true, but I have known many situations, as a police officer, where the predicament is much worse. Such scenarios do exist and human beings are doing and have always done crazy things. Women are, in fact, sleeping around with both sexes, as are men, and women are cheating just as men are.

Excuses for bad behavior, character flaws and unethical acts need not be tolerated, so set your standards high. If you find yourself in a hurtful predicament, ask yourself questions about your personal motivations instead of making nonsensical excuses. If you choose to travel the path of the fool, accept the challenge, but you must also accept responsibility for the consequences. Accept the fact that you chose your path and that the only persons responsible are you and whomever went along as a participant. The reality is that you are not all that and a bag of chips, and if you were, you wouldn't be disrespecting yourself, making excuses and blaming others for your stupidity.

Now lets take the test! Choose the items that apply to you, then choose the items that apply to your significant other, or special friend. Use a separate sheet of paper and the test is available more than once. "BE COMPLETELY HONEST"!

MAINTENANCE PROFILE TEST

A).I look great

A).I am socially aware

D).I share a lot

B).I am a team player

A).I am high spirited

B).I am conceited

C).I am greedy

B).I over dress

B).Leave everything to God

C).I am inconsiderate

C).I am devious

A).I seldom make excuses

D).I am understanding

C).I play unfair

C). I am wasteful

A). I am competitive

A). I am classy

A). I am insightful

C). I play unfair

C). I am insensitive

A). I am responsible

D). I am spiritual

A). I am supportive

B). I have poor skills

C). I am cold hearted

B). I always play angles

B). I justify immoral acts

B). I am smart enough

B). I have great communication Skills

B). Someone else is always at fault

B). I rely on my good looks too much

B). I am a little dishonest.

B). I will do anything for money

B). I am a prima donna

A). I am a hard worker

D). I am financial adept

C). I am narrow minded

A). I am well educated

C). I am selfish

D). I am a good, caring lover

C). I have an addictive nature

A). I listen a lot

Calculate the number of each alphabet

A_____

B_____

C_____

D_____

Now let's develop a graph by darkening a space for each alphabet:

A	B	C	D
HIGH	LOW	HIGH	LOW
PROFILE	PROFILE	MAINTENANCE	
(12)	(12)	(12)	(12)
(11)	(11)	(11)	(11)
(10)	(10)	(10)	(10)
(9)	(9)	(9)	(9)
(8)	(8)	(8)	(8)
(7)	(7)	(7)	(7)
(6)	(6)	(6)	(6)
(5)	(5)	(5)	(5)
(4)	(4)	(4)	(4)
(3)	(3)	(3)	(3)
(2)	(2)	(2)	(2)
(1)	(1)	(1)	(1)

After the recent mayoral race in Baltimore, many Blacks debated the idea that the White Candidate ran to split the vote between Black Candidates. The reality is that he got more than the combined votes for both African American Candidates, and there were legitimate reasons. The debate continued: "He is not going to do anything about drugs and the problems that we have in our schools, because Baltimore is predominantly a "Chocolate City"! "No one, but you, is going to fix your personal problems, and you need to stop looking beyond yourself for solutions. All politicians can do is work to provide employment and business opportunities, such that you can develop sanctuary and guide those whom you love toward fulfillment. If you got anything from this book, I hope that you will seek truth and understanding; "Stop paying homage to, and gain psychological freedom from institutions and people who feel that they have a right to disrespect you. Learn to:

1. "TEACH BY EXAMPLE"! Children are the most important part of a family, not your car, your house, or your fine Clothes. If such is not the case; "Don't have children"!

2. Challenge all attempts to take advantage of you by use of politics, coersion, violence, drugs, scams, and other unethical means, because your children are watching, and they learn from you.

3. Take back our children, from, drug dealers, panderers, hustlers, weak teachers, sell out public servants and religious zealots.

4. Follow leaders who set good examples and hold them accountable. Once again "Your children are watching!".

5. Mentor discipline, morals, and standards, and grow beyond the information and rules that were your parent's, if you want to avoid confusion and communicate with, not at, your children.

6. Realize, early in the game, that parenting is a skill to be learned and not, intuition, or reflex.

7. Mentor relationship skills, acceptable manners, basic salutations and move to a higher plane, crystallize your thoughts about caring, sharing and respect.

8. Combine research with your emotions in guiding your children to a profitable future, because we exist in a capitalist, not a socialist democracy, and emotions are not enough.

9. "STOP USING GOD AS A CRUTCH", because while you do whatever you want: "YOUR CHILDREN ARE WATCHING, AND LEARNING–FROM YOU"!

Chapter 34

I have written some poems about life's realities and hope you understand the messages:

Getting paid
My morals and my standards
couldn't bring my lover down.
He's so dumb, he ran away,
Left home, he left my town.

I don't care what ere he thinks,
He doesn't understand.
I'm just concerned about myself,
shucks, I don't need a man!

After all its my body
and I'll do what ere I please.
And what's love got to do with it,
this nonsense has to cease.

He doesn't make me happy
and he can't fulfill my needs.
He doesn't make the money
so who cares about his deeds.

He says he wants a woman
that's a warm and caring wife.
So I brought him a teddy bear,
that he can hug for life.

And now I'll hug my satin sheets
my car, my fur, my gold!
I wonder why I'm lonely,
damn this empty bed is cold!

Respect

You say my understanding's bad,
that I don't comprehend.
I'm foolish, I don't care enough,
and often I offend.

My response to you is basic,
I don't like being used.
I always take good care of me,
don't act like I'm confused.

It's not my job to care for you,
though often I may share.
And though I do lot for you,
It's you, you just don't care.

You always take advantage,
and you never get enough.
You want someone to give and give,
and damn it, I say tough.

How long will you go on like this,
at what age will you learn.
Respect is not just given,
It is something you must earn.

When I was a police officer, religion was the biggest scam on the streets!
Jim Jones took hundreds of people from this country and got them to
drink poison Kool Aid using religion as a catalyst! The Branch Davidians,
Reverend Ike, Daddy Grace, Father Divine, King Narciss, Jerry Falwell,
Oral Roberts and many others should imply, to a thinking person that,
that all is not well in the world of religion.

Don't play with God
Your insides are decaying.
but your smile bright as the sun,
will fool God folks with hearts of gold,
while you are having fun.

And though you take advantage,
and play games with no concern,
for those who have much love for you;
The bridges that you burn.

Are bridges to a better life,
to needs you must fulfill.
But you don't care, you want much more
and more and more and still.

You have so much, so very much
material and things.
But there's no love, no caring,
no more friendships, no more rings.

Screw the world and make it big,
lie to your heart's content.
Once you've done your loved ones in,
religion's where you vent.

And now you turn to God,
while things you do make Satan drool.
Don't worry, do just what you want,
there'll be another fool.

You're on your way to judgment day,
to heaven you will go.
You haven't learned a blessed thing
your future's down below!

She once said that she thought that I was her soul mate. A cop and a
crook; what a team!

Love Affair (with gold)
Take it from someone who knows
and loves to give advice,
anyone who wants true love
must learn to sacrifice.

If you're not there to give your all,
to give a hundred percent,
then you're not investing dear,
you're only paying rent.

There are those who take and take
and never learn to give.
The don't enjoy much happiness
they never learn to live.

So when you look around you and
you find your life's a mess,
Ask yourself how much it took
To bury your success.

And one day when you're old and gray
the stories that are told,
will there sharing, caring, warmth
did one heart lost and cold,

Destroy what our lives could have been
for a love affair with gold.

Love games start in the bedroom, flow through church and courts and
end up in the toilet. The ultimate victims are children.

Love Games
It takes just one to ruin a group,
to halt the rise to fame.
To bring a solid family down,
it takes one ruinous game.

While one who loves, who truly loves
may never wear a crown.
Her spirit shines bright as the sun,
His soul on solid ground.

My love for you, strong as it was,
each challenge every test.
The years went by, so hard, so cold,
I hoped were not our best.

Then one day when vows were broke
we sang our parting song,
emotions flared and hearts were torn
when right lost out to wrong.

In the end I'll surely say
that I gave love my all,
but love requires hard work from two
I hope you will recall.

The many times I asked of you
the part you could have played.
in helping make our marriage strong,
responses were delayed.

And to this day I sadly say
and answer never came.
could love have grown forever strong
without that foolish game?

She had money, cars, clothes and jewelry, but never thought for a
minute about her daughter who was in college, or her son, who really

needs us. I helped pay her legal fees that were needed to win a discrimination lawsuit at her job, but when she got her settlement we got left alone. When she collected on false insurance claims, we got left out. I wrote this poem for children who need love, warmth and caring in their lives.

Katydids (candy and caring)
Do you know what Katydid?
Katy found a can and hid.
She did not go too far away.
She knew to someone's mouth she'd stray.

She's found her way into you home.
From here she'll never need to roam.
Please give her a warm caress, and
she will give you happiness.

Here's the can where Katy hid.
Please enjoy your Katydid.

The following poems reflect my respect for my family, and their efforts to do the right thing. I come from good stock and believe that many of the issues that effect Black Families are from within. Racism is a factor, but family is the foundation on which we build strong soldiers to fight injustice.

Grandma's Lead
My cousins, aunts and uncles,
all good people in my life.
The best of men, great women,
so much fun, so, little strife.

My memories of childhood,
filled with pleasantries and sharing.
Hard times always balanced,
with much loving and much caring.

I always felt the good life
was just at my fingertips.
Encouraged by the sweet words flowing
from my mothers lips.

My father was a good man,
firm example, little speech.
The insight, how to be a man,
things only he could teach.

My siblings and my cousins
and their children are a team.
Great leadership and guidance
vow to make the future gleam.

My son and my daughter,
they inherit what I know.
Be patient, feed a fertile mind,
and from there love will grow.

My nephews and my nieces,
how their efforts will be praised.
They have learned from parents.
that my generation raised.

If all will just follow Grandma's lead,
stay with the master plan.
They will climb and fall and climb,
but on their feet they'll land.

Surely in a great, great while
a few will go astray.
but they'll return, the help,
support is never far away.

The standards set by folks who knew
all that we need to learn.
That, if we strive to do good things
respect is what we earn.

So, as you look around you,
all the trouble that you see
your path is paved, your vision clear.
you're from good family!

Estelle, my grandmother, mother, aunts, sisters, cousins: all candy
ladies. After many years of driving past Estelle's Mother's Home and wanting to stop and talk, I finally did just that. Our brief conversation
reminded me of all that I was when I was with Estelle. This poem was
inspired by my Aunt Sis, but reflects the many good women in my life.

Candy Lady
Her caring and her sharing,
graying hair and tender hands.
With thoughts so pure, the love she gives
of self with no demands.

Though she was near a century old,
her heart was warm as spring.
Her twilight years, the memories,
of every smallish thing.

Her presence warmed my aging heart,
her essence laced with gold.
Her radiance, the warmth I felt,
like shelter from the cold.

When Grandma ceased at spreading love,
her daughters took the reins.
Now all, have gone, have passed away,
our losses, heavens gains.

She was spreading candy,
among all her aging friends.
Her kindness never, ever ceased
her giving never ends.

Now I have a girl child,
who is kind like my Aunt Sis.
And like the candy lady
she will settle for a kiss.

She's kind and warm and full of love
as others born before her.
My aunts, sisters, cousins with
my grandma and my mother.

I love them candy ladies all,
so dear, so kind, so sweet.
They taught me how to spread my wings,
to move beyond our street.

They are the reason I exist,
the warmth on which I soar.
I teach my child what they taught,
to spread love ever more.

At the end of the marriage I was introduced to a young lady who made me to realize that, "It's all about being happy"! She gave both a history lesson and a vision of the future. She was the end of my naivete, and the beginning of my journey toward sanctuary.

Oh but for a moment
my whole world was ablaze.
My heart filled with desire,
I was blinded by the haze.

I tasted of your nectar,
oh so hot and such a thrill.
I know I should have waited,
but I moved in for the kill.

And in those fleeting moments,
my dreams I thought were true.
I feasted on desire and
the essence that was you.

Then quickly I awakened
to find I was alone.
Your flame I must have taken,
the fire, it was all gone?

Can it be rekindled,
the warmth that was your soul.
I knew I should have waited,
because now I feel the cold.

As the dew of morning
fades with the rising sun.
Can my presence build a fire
and will I walk, or run.

Will I be ever cautious, or
will I know only fear.
When once again a flame burns,
will I come so near.

Will I make a fool of self
and blunder, and offend, or
Shall I rush into the fire
and cause the flame to end.

The next poem reflects my life with Estelle, and the transition to Edita.

I may not meet your standards,
the image that I sell.
But if you'll stop and listen,
there's a story that I Tell.
About my trip to heaven

with an angel named Estelle".
It was she who taught me
to go on with my life.
To set aside my many fears
and then to take a wife.

Estelle watched over me for many years and only left me when she
knew that I had grown

At my desk I saw her face
and it took me to a place.
Where I felt her warm caress
and my check against her breast.

Though we were so far apart,
she was always in my heart.
Her smile warm, her eyes so bright,
lit my world when late at night.

Once so often in her arms
and enchanted by her charm,.
in my heart she'll always stay
she is never far away!

Estelle was a loving woman with eyes bright as stars, a heart warm as
spring, and love soft as a summer breeze. In Edita I found what Estelle
taught was good for me, I found a sweetheart: and "I found sanctuary".

End

0-595-21865-2